CUPS of LIGHT
and OTHER ILLUSTRATIONS

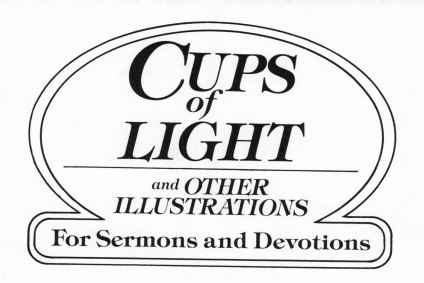

CUPS of LIGHT

and OTHER ILLUSTRATIONS

For Sermons and Devotions

Clarence W. Cranford
Foreword by Jimmy Carter

Judson Press® Valley Forge

CUPS OF LIGHT . . . AND OTHER ILLUSTRATIONS

Copyright © 1988
Judson Press, Valley Forge, PA 19482-0851

Unless otherwise indicated, Bible quotations in this volume are from the Revised Standard Version of the Bible, copyrighted 1946, 1952 © 1971, 1973 by the Division of Christian Education of the National Council of the Churches of Christ in the U.S.A, and used by permission.

Other quotations of the Bible are from

The Holy Bible, King James Version.

GOOD NEWS BIBLE, The Bible in Today's English Version. Copyright © American Bible Society, 1976. Used by permission.

The New Testament in Modern English, rev. ed. Copyright © J. B. Phillips 1972. Used by permission of the Macmillan Company and Geoffrey Bles, Ltd.

The Living Bible, Tyndale House Publishers, Wheaton, Ill. Used by permission.

LIBRARY OF CONGRESS
Library of Congress Cataloging-in-Publication Data

Cranford, Clarence W. (Clarence William), b. 1906.
    Cups of light—and other illustrations / by Clarence W. Cranford.
        p.   cm.
    ISBN 0-8170-1142-0
    1. Meditations.   2. Homiletical illustrations.   I. Title.
BV4832.2.C69   1988
251'.08—dc19   88-9044
                                                                     CIP

The name JUDSON PRESS is registered as a trademark in the U.S. Patent Office.
Printed in the U.S.A.

JIMMY CARTER

22 December 1987

Among the many bright spots in my life as President of the United States was attending First Baptist Church in Washington with Dr. Clarence Cranford as our pastor. His sermons were always inspirational and entertaining, even enough to keep the attention of Amy and her early teenage friends riveted on the pulpit.

Cranny was always able to use his own experiences and his remarkable insight into the life and teachings of Christ to drive home lessons that were timely for our family and the other worshipers. During these same times, his gentleness, scholarship, and sensitivity made his personal counseling invaluable to us.

After returning to Plains, we continued to benefit from the close friendship of Cranny and Dorothy. One of the more memorable experiences was their visit to our home and Cranny's preaching in our small Maranatha Baptist Church. On this occasion I urged him to write another book and, half facetiously, he said he would do so if I would write a brief foreword. Recognizing a good bargain, I immediately agreed. He sent me the manuscript a few months later. However, before a publisher could be chosen, we learned that our friend's life on earth was over.

This book will be another valuable legacy of this remarkable minister of the gospel. Those of us who knew and loved Cranny are delighted that it will be published; other readers will understand why his memory is so dear to us.

Jimmy Carter

To my children and grandchildren

Preface

Why don't you publish a book of illustrations?"

This question was put to me by some students in the Southern Baptist Theological Seminary at Louisville, after I had delivered a series of lectures on preaching. Others who have heard me preach, including many of my clergy friends, have made the same suggestion.

One suggestion went further. "Why don't you," asked one friend, "add a brief message to each illustration so you can help us to see what the illustration illustrates?"

This suggestion appealed to me. After all, even Jesus sometimes had to explain some of his parables before his hearers could grasp their meaning. Even so obvious a parable as the story of the sower had to be explained to the disciples (Luke 8:9).

So this I decided to do. For over half a century I have sought to proclaim the good news of God's purpose and love which I believe was supremely revealed in Jesus Christ. In those years, I have used many illustrations and told many experiences to give added illumination to what I was trying to say. Illustrations can serve as windows to let in more light on the subject being considered. They have great recall value. People can easily remember a vivid illustration and thus are helped to remember the truth that was being illustrated.

The illustrations in this book deal with the Christian life. They begin with Jesus who is "the pioneer and perfecter" of the Christian faith (Hebrews 12:2). They stress the need for inner renewal and the role of the Holy Spirit in helping us gain such renewal. They stress the importance of Christian growth and some of the aids that can help us achieve that growth. They proceed, as all Christian experience should, to the urgency of Christian outreach and service to others, and they end with suggestions for joyous and dynamic Christian living.

The messages are reminders that some phase of God's truth can be seen everywhere because God is everywhere. Some cups of light or glimpses of God's truth, therefore, can be seen everywhere if we have the eyes to see them. God's truth is written in the stars, but it can also be seen in the common occurrences of everyday life. It can be seen in a picture of a father leading his child by the hand, in a cartoon of an impious boy squirting a water pistol at Niagara Falls, in an unusual Mother's Day card, and even in a car thief's incredible experience. These are only a few of the many places where this book can help you to catch a fresh glimpse of God's truth.

I wish to thank Miss Evelyn Baumgartner for typing, and retyping, this manuscript. For many years she served as a leading and invaluable member of the staff of Calvary Baptist Church in Washington, D. C. I also wish to thank Mrs. Charles Morgan, an active member of the First Baptist Church of that city, for some additional typing of the manuscript when I was serving as the interim pulpit minister of that historic church.

And, of course, I am deeply humbled and honored by former president Jimmy Carter's willingness to write the foreword for this book. For a while it was my great privilege to have President and Mrs. Carter and their daughter Amy in the congregation to which I preached. My heart swells with pride when I think of their outstanding Christian witness, and of the way it shone so brightly when they lived in the White House.

With the inspiration of their friendship and the leading of God's Holy Spirit, I invite you to look with me at some glimpses of God's truth that can deepen our faith and lead us to greater joy and triumph in our Christian living.

Clarence W. Cranford

Contents

1

The Supremacy of Jesus

This book begins where Christianity begins—with Jesus Christ. After all, he is the "Alpha and Omega, the beginning and the ending" of the Christian faith (Revelation 1:8, KJV). To know him is to know the character and purpose of God. We know what God is trying to say to us through the Bible, because we know Jesus. The Old Testament anticipates him. The New Testament presents and interprets him. The Bible does not give us a set of rules to follow slavishly, but a person to follow faithfully and lovingly. Jesus not only knows the way to God. As he himself reminds us, he *is* the way to God. To follow him is to walk in deeper fellowship with God.

To some it may seem strange that the great eternal God of the universe would be revealed in such a humble, human way. Whoever would have guessed, for example, that when God's truth concerning God's redemptive purpose for humankind was to be most fully revealed, it would be through a person who lived as a humble carpenter and teacher? Who would have suspected that we would meet God through a cross that would fulfill rather than thwart God's plan, and through a tomb that could not hold its prey?

God's love and purpose for humankind are so fully revealed in the life, death, and resurrection of Jesus that not all our glimpses added together can ever enable us fully to fathom its meaning or plumb its mystery. We can only stand in utter awe at the "breadth and length and height and depth" of God's love and power as seen through the life and ministry of Jesus (Ephesians 3:18).

Nevertheless, we can always hope that each new experience will give us some new personal glimpse of God's love, some new awareness of God's nearness, some new reminder of God's will for our lives. Nothing can do this better than illustrations that turn our attention to the life and ministry of Jesus. Let us then look at some of these brief messages that serve as windows through which we can catch some important glimpses of Jesus' significance for our day.

Niagara Falls and Water Pistols

One of my favorite cartoons shows a boy standing in the very front of the boat called *The Maid of the Mist.* This is the boat that carries sightseers so close to Niagara Falls that they must wear raingear to keep from being drenched by the spray. Wearing his raincoat and hat, the boy is standing in the front of the boat, and guess what he is doing! He is squirting a water pistol at Niagara Falls.

People can be like that. They can aim criticisms at the Bible. Nevertheless, in the light of the Bible's continuing witness to the righteousness and love of God, any attempt to discredit its message is like squirting a water pistol at Niagara Falls.

So it is when we try to understand God's nature by human reason. Intelligence is one of God's greatest gifts to humankind. By intelligence, people have built civilizations, created art, and penetrated some of the mysteries of the universe. But all efforts to comprehend the nature and purpose of God by human reason are like mere drops from a water pistol compared to the Niagara-like revelation that streams from Christ and his cross.

So it is, too, with our faith in immortality. Many comforting reasons have been advanced to assure us of life after death, but all our efforts to convince ourselves of life beyond the grave are mere dribbles compared to the Niagara of assurance that cascades from Jesus' resurrection.

We need to put away our little water pistols of doubt and despair and to look again at the Niagara of love and hope that flows from Jesus' life, death, and resurrection.

Down to What?

A father was telling his son about mythology. According to ancient mythology, he explained, the world was held on the shoulders of a god named Atlas. He, in turn, was supported on the back of a giant turtle, and the turtle was supported by several elephants, one on top of the other.

"But what was the bottom elephant on?" asked the boy.

"Another elephant," replied the father.

"But, Dad," asked the boy, "what was *it* on?"

"Son," replied the father, "there were elephants all the way down."

But down to what? That is the question. And the same question may be asked concerning the Christian faith. On what is it based? Speculation? Wishful thinking? Philosophical reasoning?

The Christian faith is based on a revelation that came through an actual life, and through actual events that happened in that life. It is based on the life, death, and resurrection of Jesus. We can deny an argument, but we cannot deny the concreteness of Jesus' life and example.

Jesus is the foundation of our faith because his life was the perfect fulfillment of Old Testament prophecy. Paul could say, "Christ died for our sins . . . was buried . . . and was raised on the third day . . . in accordance with the scriptures" (1 Corinthians 15:3-4). We know where the Old Testament is pointing because we know Jesus. Without him the Bible contains much inspiration and good advice. With him at the center, it becomes the good news of God's love in Christ.

Jesus is the foundation of our faith because he lived in perfect obedience to God. His entire life, therefore, reveals the will and purpose of God.

Jesus is the foundation of our faith because his resurrection gives validity to everything he said. We can believe him when he promises eternal life, because he rose from the dead.

A Constant in the Midst of Change

A friend was speaking to a man who had lived to a ripe old age. "You've seen a lot of changes in your time," said the friend. "Yep," said the old man, "and I've been agin them all."

There have always been changes, many of them quite drastic. Our ancestors saw the transition from kerosene lamps to electric lights; from horse-and-buggy days to transportation by auto and airplane. They saw the coming of the telephone and radio. It is hard for people today to feel the impact these drastic changes have brought about in the lifestyle of the people who lived through them.

In our lifetime we have seen such new things as the atomic bomb, television, tape recorders, supermarkets, computers, condominiums, stereos, jet propulsion, traffic jams, rock and roll music, X-rated movies, runaway inflation, and many more. No wonder someone has said that even the future isn't what it used to be.

And yet some things remain the same. People still get hungry and need food. They still experience grief and need to be comforted. They still become confused and need guidance. They still get lonely and need to feel that somebody cares. They still sin and need forgiveness. They still get older and need to make adjustments. They still die and need a message of hope.

Fortunately, God's love hasn't changed. The love that was revealed in Jesus remains the same, for Christ is "the same yesterday and today and forever" (Hebrews 13:8). Time cannot erode his image, nor can it lessen his power. To those in darkness, Christ is God's light. To those looking for life's meaning, he is God's truth. To those who feel rejected, he is God's invitation to come home. To those who face death, he is God's proof of eternal life. In the midst of the waves of change, he is our constant, our North Star.

The Superstar Syndrome

Jesus Christ, Superstar! A few decades ago these words were emblazoned across the entertainment pages of our newspapers when a musical show bearing that title became popular. The humble Galilean's life has been dramatized in many forms over the years on Broadway and on the silver screen. The one who said "I am meek and lowly in heart" has often been turned into a box-office attraction.

There is some good in this phenomenon. It captures the attention of some who are turned off by traditional approaches. To them, perhaps for the first time in their lives, Jesus emerges as a real person. They sense something of the inner struggle that must have gone on in Judas, and in Mary Magdalene, and in Jesus himself as he neared his death.

But there is a danger in such presentations. Jesus is not a superstar; he is the world's Savior. To think of Bruce Springsteen or Martina Navratilova or Luciano Pavarotti as superstars is to elevate them to a high position. But to think of Jesus as a superstar is to demote him from his rightful position as the son of God.

Moreover, there is a greater danger. The role of superstars is to entertain. We are mere spectators who enjoy their performances. But if Jesus Christ is the "Lamb of God, who takes away the sin of the world" (John 1:29), we are *involved.* We are the lost that he came to save. We must come to him not for entertainment but for eternal life; not to enjoy his performance but to seek his pardon and peace.

If Jesus Christ is only a superstar, we can enjoy him. But if he is our Savior, we must obey him. He does not want us to applaud him but to emulate him; not to give him a standing ovation but to give him our heart's devotion. He does not want us to be moved to cheers but to repentance; not to be thrilled but to be transformed; not to sway to the beat of music but to respond to his marching orders.

In the end, he offers what no mere superstar ever can. He offers us forgiveness and eternal life. He is not a figure behind the lights. He is the Way, the Truth, and the Life.

The Debt We Owe

On the evening of May 25, 1977, a great crowd of people, including many notables, gathered in Carnegie Hall in New York City to honor the great singer Marian Anderson, and to see her receive three awards: one from New York City presented by the mayor, one from the United Nations presented by an officer of that international body, and one from the United States, a resolution of appreciation adopted unanimously by both houses of Congress, presented by the then First Lady, Mrs. Jimmy Carter.

The evening's program was brought to a close with three songs sung by Leontyne Price. Before singing them, Miss Price paid a personal tribute to Miss Anderson. "My dear, beloved Marian Anderson," she said, "because *you* were, *I* am." In other words, the fact that Marian Anderson had succeeded in breaking the color barrier many years earlier had made it easier for Leontyne Price to be accepted as a black artist. In the same way, all black athletes today can say of the pioneer black baseball player, Jackie Robinson, "Because you were, I am."

Think of all the people to whom we are indebted for being what we are today. Of course, we can say to our parents, "Because you were, I am." But think of the teachers to whom we can say, "Because you were, I am a better educated person," or the doctors to whom we can say, "Because you were, I am well." Think of many people who opened doors for us, to whom we can say, "Because of you, I was able to move ahead."

Most of all, we can say to Jesus, "Because you were, and are, and evermore will be, I am able to turn to God with new confidence in his forgiveness and acceptance. Because of you, I can face life with a new purpose, and I can face death with a new hope."

Strange Gifts for a Baby

When Prince Charles was born in England, he received several trainloads of gifts. The list, published at the time, was incredible. Every toy manufacturer in the world, plus heads of state and many others, must have sent him a gift. For this was no ordinary baby. He was born to be a king.

When Jesus was born, he received three gifts: gold, frankincense, and myrrh. They were strange gifts for a baby, but very appropriate for this particular baby, for in addition to their practical value, they had a special meaning.

The gold represents his kingship. Gold was given to a child who was expected to be a king, and this child was expected to become king of the Jews. Jesus was later to make it clear that he did not come to rule over a political kingdom, but over a spiritual one (John 18:36). In God's spiritual kingdom, he is the king of kings, and as such, deserves to rule in our hearts.

The frankincense reminds us that he is also lord of lords, for frankincense was used in worship. It therefore represents his deity. When you add all the human factors together, you still have not explained Jesus. He himself explained his life by its relationships to the Father (John 10:30; 14:9-11). His claims would have been incredible, were it not for his life and resurrection. His resurrection gives validity to every claim he ever made.

The third gift was the strangest of all to give a baby, for myrrh was used to anoint the bodies of the dead. It was as if, by this gift, the wise men were saying, "This baby was born to die." Apart from his life, his death would have had no meaning. But apart from his death, his mission would have been incomplete. By his life he became our perfect example, but by his death he became our all-sufficient Savior.

Silver Goblets and China Teacups

It was Communion Sunday. Before me on the Communion table were trays of highly polished silver and a shining silver goblet. All the trays and the goblet had been lovingly repolished after every use. The gleaming silver was a symbol of our desire to use only the best in our service of God.

But something about it bothered me. I was sure that the cup from which Jesus and the disciples drank at the last supper was not made of silver. More likely, it was an ordinary earthenware cup such as a poor man might use on his table. An ordinary teacup, I thought, would be a more accurate symbol of the One who, though he "thought it not robbery to be equal with God," nevertheless *emptied himself,* and took upon himself "the form of a servant" (Philippians 2:7, KJV).

Moreover, as Paul so graphically expressed it, though we contain the priceless treasure of Christ's redeeming love, we ourselves are like mere "earthen vessels" (2 Corinthians 4:7). So as I rose to lead in the Lord's Supper, I lifted up an ordinary teacup that I had brought from the church kitchen. Quoting Philippians 2:7, I poured the contents of the silver goblet into the cup. Then quoting 2 Corinthians 4:7, I held up the cup before the congregation, and as they drank from glasses lifted from the trays, I drank from the ordinary cup.

In this way I tried to symbolize the incarnation in which God's eternal nature was poured into human flesh, and also to remind us that God has entrusted the glorious truth of the gospel to us who are earthen vessels at best.

How Far Can You Jump?

A minister in Iowa was preaching on the text, "I can do all things in him who strengthens me" (Philippians 4:13). What, he wondered, could he say or do in the children's sermon to help the boys and girls understand the meaning of that verse?

Finally, he got an idea. He lined the children up in front of one of the front pews and told them to jump across the aisle so they would be in front of the pew on the other side of the aisle. Of course, none of them could jump that far. They could jump one foot, two feet, even three feet, but not all the way across the aisle.

When he came to the last little girl, he told her to count to three and jump. Then he put his hands under her armpits, and as she jumped, he lifted her and carried her across the aisle. "See," he said, "she did it." "No," said the children, "you helped her. You carried her."

Then he explained: "That's the way it is with us. We can't jump out of our sins but Jesus can lift us out of our sins. We can't jump into the presence of God, but Jesus can lift us into the presence of God. We can't jump into heaven, but, when the time comes, Jesus can lift us into heaven. We can't jump out of our selfishness and fears, but, if we let him, Jesus can lift us out of our selfishness and fears."

Before he wrote the words of the text, Paul told us, "Whatever is true . . . honorable . . . just . . . pure . . . lovely . . . gracious . . . *think* about these things" (Philippians 4:8). He knew the power of "positive thinking." But he did not go on to say, "I can do all things through my thoughts which strengthen me." He knew, and so do we, that often our thoughts are not as true, honorable, just, pure, lovely, and gracious, as we know they ought to be. We need help, and Jesus can give us that help.

Let's show the world how far we can jump—when we let Jesus lift us.

Empty Words or Valid Promise?

In what is said to be a true incident in the life of Abraham Lincoln, a group of men once went to the White House to urge him to issue an emancipation proclamation that would free the slaves. But Lincoln felt that the time was not yet ripe for such a move. So he asked the men, "How many legs will a sheep have if you call the tail a leg?"

Naturally, they answered, "Five." "No," said Mr. Lincoln, "calling the tail a leg will not make it so." His point was that a mere statement on a piece of paper would not free the slaves. He felt he had to wait until the military situation gave promise of making such an edict work.

Just wishing something were so does not make it so. A diploma hanging on a wall does not ensure a lifetime of success. Only integrity and hard work can do that. A marriage certificate cannot guarantee a happy home. Only love and fidelity can do that. A certificate of church membership does not make a Christian. Only loyalty to Christ can do that.

The Bible keeps saying this over and over again. "What good would it do," asks Micah, "to perform impressive acts of worship unless one is willing to do justly, and to love mercy, and to walk humbly with one's God?" "What good would it do," asks Jesus, "to bring one's gift to God's altar if one is not willing to seek reconciliation with one who is estranged from him?" "What good would it do," asks Paul, "to perform spectacular acts of charity if one does not give the gift of love along with them?"

One thing we know. When Jesus promises to free us from sin, his promise is not mere empty words. By his cross he demonstrated the reality of God's love. By his resurrection he demonstrated God's power over death. His life, his death, and his resurrection back up his claim to be our Savior. He speaks knowing that all the forces of God are on his side. That is why he could say, "If the Son makes you free, you will be free indeed" (John 8:36).

For What Will You Be Remembered?

Samuel Pepys, the English diarist, chose a bizarre way to be remembered. He left a library of three thousand volumes to Magdalene (pronounced Maudlin) College with the provision that the books must be kept in the exact order in which he left them. To make sure the provision would be carried out, his will required that once each year a committee from Trinity College must inspect the library. If any books were found to be out of place, Trinity would get the library. Then presumably, Magdelene College would appoint a committee to try to get it back.

What a ludicrous way to try to be remembered. Didn't Samuel Pepys know that future generations would ridicule this requirement? If a person wants to be remembered, surely he can think up a better way than that.

Most people who are remembered in later years were too busy in their lifetime doing something worthwhile to care whether they were remembered or not. Take Andrew, for example. He did not have the dramatic qualities of his brother Simon, but almost every time we read of him, he is bringing someone to Jesus. Now that is something worth remembering about a person.

First it was his own brother Simon (John 1:40-41). Then it was the lad with the five loaves and two fishes (John 6:8-9). Again, it was the Greeks who came looking for Jesus (John 12:21-22). The first introduction led Simon to become Peter the Apostle. The second led to the feeding of the multitudes. The third led Jesus to say, "And I, when I am lifted up from the earth will draw all men to myself" (John 12:32).

Who cares about the order of books on a shelf when he can draw others closer to Jesus? One does not need a committee to examine the bequest of God's love. The changed lives of millions show the importance of being drawn into close proximity to Jesus.

The Lord and Master of Us All

In a very old book of addresses delivered in memory of Abraham Lincoln to the Minnesota Commandery of the Loyal Legion of the United States, one of the speakers, Dr. Edward Ingersoll, tells of a time during the Civil War when armies of the Union and Confederate forces were camped on opposite sides of the Rappahannock River. They were close enough to hear each other's bands. One evening the Union band played "Rally 'Round the Flag, Boys." The Confederate band countered by playing "Way Down South in Dixie." The Union band next played "The Star Spangled Banner," to which the Confederate band responded by playing "Bonnie Blue Flag." The Yankee band then played "Hail Columbia, Happy Land," and the Confederate band answered with "Maryland, My Maryland."

As darkness began to settle on the land, the Union band began to play "Home, Sweet Home." Suddenly those who were listening realized that the Southern band had caught up the tune, and both bands were playing the same song together. Divided by political animosities, they were united in their love and yearning for home.

When it comes to doctrine and church government, churches play different tunes. Some follow time-honored practices of liturgy; others prefer to improvise with more spontaneity and informality in worship. Some stress the authority of the church, others the autonomy of the local congregation. Some stress the importance of silence, others the importance of the baptism of the Holy Spirit. Some have bishops, others elders, presbyters, or deacons. But all of them can unite in a song in praise of Jesus.

Jesus is our captain. He is our leader. He is the one we serve "whate'er our name or sign." To him we look for truth. In him we see our perfect example.

2
Messages of the Cross

The cross bothers me."

This statement was made to me with some vehemence by a young woman in whose church I had spoken.

"The cross bothers everyone who thinks about it seriously," I agreed, "for nothing in all history judges our sinfulness, our self-centeredness, our unwillingness to sacrifice as does the cross. And this," I added, "is surely as God meant it to be."

"But that isn't what I mean," she responded. "What I mean is this. If God is God, and if he wanted to forgive my sins, why didn't he just go ahead and forgive them? Why was it necessary for Jesus to die on a cross before God could, or would, forgive my sins?"

I found that her concept of the cross gave her a disturbing idea of God. She understood the cross to mean that God was so outraged by our sins that an innocent third party had to suffer and die before God's anger could be appeased. "I don't like that kind of God," she said. I replied, "I don't either, and I don't think anyone would. But if I understand my Bible," I said, "that isn't the way it happened at all."

I explained to her that people have been trying to answer her question ever since Jesus was crucified. I also reminded her that not everyone interprets the meaning of the cross in the same way. Some claim that the significance of the cross is to be seen only in its moral influence, which it certainly exerts. "But," I said, "if the message of the incarnation is true, the meaning of the cross goes much deeper than that."

Then I gave her my answer to her question.

"There are some things," I said, "that God can't do. God can do nothing that is contrary to divine nature. Any such contradiction would cause us to lose our understanding of God as revealed in Jesus. We would cease to have a God we can love and trust. That means God can never look lightly on sin or treat sin as if it did not matter. That would be contrary to divine nature, since God demands utter righteousness. Therefore, knowing that we are separated from God by our sin and by the demands of divine righteousness, God could have accepted that separation as a just punishment for us and let us go out into eternity without hope.

"But God couldn't do that either. Such a course of action would have been contrary to divine nature, for God loves us. So, prompted by love, God was clothed in human flesh and was nailed to a cross by cruel and wicked men. Thereby, through the anguish and agony of the cross, God in Christ *took on himself* the penalty of our sins. Now he is free to offer us full and complete forgiveness without having ignored or compromised his righteousness one whit.

"If this is true," I added, "as I believe it to be true, that means that God took the risk that the one in whom he clothed himself would see the divine purpose, and would be 'obedient unto death, even death on the cross' " (Philippians 2:8)

Our acceptance with God is therefore made possible not only by the love of God, but also by the obedience of Jesus. Jesus could have said No in the Garden of Gethsemane, but he said Yes and thereby fulfilled God's purpose and plan by offering himself for the sins of the world.

Though not everyone may interpret the cross in just the same way, every Christian will surely agree that somehow the cross is indispensable to God's plan for the redemption of humankind. So let us look at some illustrations and their brief messages that will turn our attention back to a hill where God's truth was written in blood.

Someone Died—for You

According to the book *A Man Called Intrepid,* during World War II Eleanor Roosevelt carried the following poem in her purse:

> Dear Lord,
> Lest I continue
> My complacent way,
> Help me to remember
> Somewhere out there
> A man died for me today.
> As long as there be war,
> I then must ask and answer,
> Am I worth dying for?

This is a question we all need to ask in the light of those who have died in order that we might enjoy freedom. Does the way we use that freedom justify such a great sacrifice?

But there is a deeper question. The Bible tells me that Jesus died for me. Am I worthy such a matchless sacrifice?

As I look at my life, I can only say, "No, I am not worthy." And yet!

And yet Jesus must have felt I was worth dying for, or he would not have died for me. In the light of that fact, how can I—how can anyone—ever continue to be complacent concerning God's love, and concerning the need of others to see that love reflected in us?

Unanswered Questions and Unsilenced Songs

I saw it in the study of the Rev. Carl Brown, pastor of the University Baptist Church in Columbus, Ohio. The sign said, "A bird does not sing because it has an answer, but because it has a song."

At first, I was puzzled by its meaning. Then I saw that it expressed my case exactly. I had just lost a loved one. I did not know why God had taken her. But, thanks to my faith, I still had a song in my heart.

I will go to my grave not knowing why some people are taken and others are left, not knowing why there is so much suffering in the world, not knowing why God permits so much evil to exist.

But of two things I am certain. This gives me my song.

Because of the cross, I know that God understands our suffering. God is not absent from us, looking on human suffering in an impersonal way from some celestial height. God understands our suffering because of the anguish of seeing the undeserved agony of Christ on the cross. In fact, if what Christians believe about the incarnation is true, God was in that suffering. God understands our suffering, because God has suffered.

Second, the cross did not defeat God. It became the instrument of our redemption, and the gateway to the resurrection. And your death, or mine, will not defeat God either. The One who raised Christ from the dead will keep the promise that we also will inherit eternal life.

So I am not a Christian because I know all the answers. I am a Christian because, through knowing Christ, I know that God loves me and that Christ died for me. I know too that I have his promise that one day I shall be where he is. That is my song.

The Measure of Success

The minister of a large American church was visiting overseas, and was invited to speak to a small Christian group. In the course of his remarks, he boasted about the size of his church in America. "We have a church of two thousand members," he boasted. "Why, we even have two hundred people in prayer meeting every week." When he finished, a man stood up and said, "I suggest we have a season of prayer for our brother and his church. They have eighteen hundred members who do not go to prayer meeting."

It all depends on how we look at things. What seems like success to us may not seem like success to God. God measures success by a different yardstick. We are impressed by numbers. God is impressed by the measure of our faith. We are impressed by size. God is impressed by our trust. We are impressed by appearance. God is impressed by how much love we have for others. Our willingness to reach out to one person in need may be more important to God than the ability to sway the multitudes.

Americans worship success, and they define success in worldly terms. Prominent position. Large income. Social standing. Of course, these are not always bad—the world needs great and prominent leaders—but, as Jesus pointed out, these must never be our primary goals.

The cross was hardly the biggest success story of the first century. Measured in terms of worldly success, it was a dismal failure. But, measured in terms of God's plan, it is one of the greatest success stories of all time. Only the story of the resurrection tops it. What the world considered a failure was God's great success.

Lost and Found

Have you ever seen a child lost from its mother in a large department store? It is a sight to clutch at one's heart. Suddenly the child's secure little world has been shattered. The child is alone in a vast and confusing world.

I saw such a child recently. The child panicked. He ran to and fro, convulsively crying for his mother.

Suddenly a store employee was on her knees before him. She put her arms around him. In a tender and loving way, she tried to assure him that they would find his mother.

She had resources the child could not guess. She had a public address system over which she could announce the child's plight. If worse came to worst, she could appeal through the police radio for help.

We live in a vast and confusing world. We hardly know which way to turn. We feel like a child lost from its parents.

But one day Jesus came. He assured us that God is a loving parent, is looking for us, and wants our broken relationships to be restored so that we will no longer feel lost and cut off from the One who loves us.

Imagine the child's relief—and the parent's—when they were reunited. Both were frantic till they found each other. The cross reveals the amazing greatness of the love of God, the extent to which God would go to find us. It assures us that long before we started looking for God, God was looking for us.

Oh, the joy of being found!

How Confused Are You?

In his book *Boston Ways, High, By, and Folk,* George Weston, Jr. says: "The geographical center of Boston is in Roxbury—at the corner of Westminster and Walnut Avenues, if one cares to be precise. Due north of the center, we find the South End. This is not to be confused with South Boston, which lies directly east from South End. North of South Boston is East Boston and southwest of that is the North End."

If that doesn't confuse a person, nothing will. We live in a confused and confusing world. It's a world in which some people in Washington, D. C. held a *cocktail party* to raise money for the treatment of alcoholics; where the only effective way to maintain peace seems to be to prepare for war; where people cry out against governmental interference but in the same breath cry out for government subsidies. One would think that all nations would see the sanity of disarmament and cooperation. But they are like the people who begged Jesus to go away after he had healed a man who had been sorely possessed. They were afraid of sanity, because their priorities were wrong. They put pigs ahead of people (Matthew 8:28-34).

As one reads about the last days of Jesus' life, one is impressed by his calmness in the midst of the growing confusion around him. While others were losing their heads, he kept his. Judas might lose his loyalty, Peter his courage, the Sanhedrin its sense of justice, Pilate his ability to make his own decisions, the crowd its sensitivity to human suffering, the soldiers their humaneness, but Jesus maintained his dignity to the end. To Pilate's threats, he spoke of God's truth. To the childishness of Herod, he responded with silence. He thought of the future welfare of his mother. He prayed for his tormenters. He, not they, gave the impression of being in command of the situation. In the midst of those confused, Jesus remained calm.

A Study in Pronouns

The women's liberation movement has turned the spotlight on pronouns. Use the pronoun "he," and understandably the feminine half of the world feels left out. And yet in a male-dominated world, references to God have invariably been in the masculine gender. Before their child was born, one couple referred to their unborn child as "herm." Perhaps we need such a pronoun to indicate that God transcends all human differences.

But other pronouns are important, too. We use "I" too often, when we should say "we." We use "my" when we should say "our."

It was Dr. Carlyle Marney who suggested that we pay special attention to the pronouns when we read the 53rd chapter of Isaiah. It helps to bring out the meaning of this great chapter.

The predominant pronoun is "he." "*He* was despised and rejected by men." "*He* has borne our griefs, and carried our sorrows." "*He* was bruised for our iniquities." "*He* was oppressed, and *he* was afflicted."

Who was *he?* Only one person fulfills this prophecy in every respect, and that person is Jesus.

But who did these terrible things to him? *We* did. "*We* esteemed him not." "All *we* like sheep have gone astray." "We have turned everyone to his own way." In other words, we are the kind of people who crucified Jesus. We share in their sins.

Why did Jesus let these things happen? He did it for *our* sakes. "He has borne *our* griefs, and carried *our* sorrows." "He was wounded for *our* transgressions."

Where was God in all this? In the preceding chapter, God speaks of "*my* servant." And at the conclusion of Chapter 53 God says, "Therefore *I* will divide him a portion with the great." God was in the beginning and at the ending. God was in and through it all. And God did it all for *us.*

You Ain't Carrying No Cross

The following human interest item appeared in a Los Angeles newspaper on the day after Easter a few years ago. A cab driver decided he did not want to get caught in the traffic jam of people going to the Hollywood Bowl for the Easter sunrise service, so he parked his cab and went into a diner for a cup of coffee. A drunken man was in the diner, and seeing the driver wearing his cab operator's cap, the drunk asked him to take him out to the sunrise service.

Looking at the drunk with surprise, the cab driver said, *"You* want to go there! Why?" "Well," said the man, "everybody's going." The cab driver said, "Well, Bud, you ain't. And I'll tell you why you ain't. You gotta carry a cross to go out there, and you ain't carrying no cross."

As one looks at the church today, one gets the impression that not too many people, even among those who call themselves Christians, are carrying a cross that is costing them very much.

I don't mean that there are no Christians who are carrying heavy burdens. Christians are not exempt from suffering. They suffer pain and grief as much as anybody else. They too can suffer financial reverses and serious illness. They too face the inevitability of death. But these are crises that all people face.

A cross, as Jesus meant it, definitely means self-denial. "If any man would come after me, *let him deny himself* and take up his cross and follow me" (Matthew 16:24).

A cross means that one believes so much in something that one commits self, talents, time, and money to its furtherance. It means helping to bear another's burden.

This is the kind of discipleship to which Jesus calls us. Even the church itself must shoulder a cross on behalf of the needy, the oppressed, the sinful. In this way the cross of discipleship can reflect in a small way the cross of redemption that Jesus bore.

Nailed to the Cross

In her excellent autobiography entitled *My Life,* former Israeli prime minister Golda Meir tells about her devout Jewish grandfather who lived in Russia. For sixteen years he was required to serve in the Russian army. During all that time, in spite of ridicule and harassment, he tried faithfully to keep every Jewish law and custom.

Even so, for the rest of his life after he returned home from the army, he slept every night on a stone floor with a stone for a pillow to try to atone for any sins he might inadvertently have committed.

One cannot laugh at such devotion to one's faith, or make fun of such a drastic effort to try to win acceptance with God. But, in the light of the Christian gospel, how tragic! For, when we turn to God through faith in Christ, the New Testament assures us that God forgives all our sins, for God took away that which condemns us, "nailing it to the cross" (Colossians 2:14).

God does not ask for self-abasement, but for self-surrender; not for self-inflicted torture, but for God-directed trust. Even if we did everything we could think of to try to atone for our own sins, we would still fall far short of the perfection God wants to see in us. Only Christ could atone for the sins of others, for only he had no sins of his own that needed atonement. And what only he could do, he has done for us, so we can accept his atonement and try to show our gratitude by living gladly for God.

Not a stone pillow, but a surrendered heart. Not a cold floor that invites arthritis, but a glad faith that proclaims the wonder of God's forgiving love. This is what we need.

Across and Up and Down

I am a crossword puzzle fan. I enjoy filling in the squares with the proper letters. Often I cannot guess the horizontal word until the vertical word gives me a clue. Sometimes it is the other way around.

So it is with the Christian faith. It has both a vertical and a horizontal dimension. It reaches up in faith to God. It reaches out in love to one's neighbor. Nothing less can give a satisfactory answer to the puzzling problems of life.

The cross is our constant reminder. It has both a vertical and a horizontal part. It illustrates both upreach and outreach. Dr. Richard Roberts says this is shown by Jesus' first and last words from the cross. The first word, he says, in which Jesus prayed for his tormentors, reveals a "love that would not let go of man." And the last word, "Into thy hands I commend my spirit," reveals a "faith that would not let go of God."

We need both if we are to fill the empty places in life. They interlock with each other. The fact that I believe God has forgiven my sins makes me want to be a more forgiving person. And the fact that others have forgiven me when I have hurt or offended them helps me more fully to understand God's forgiveness for my life.

We must pray for both upward vision and outward compassion as we seek to solve the puzzling problems of life.

Mudflats and Moonbeams

On a university campus Dr. Halford Luccock was leading a discussion of religion. One student who disagreed with what Dr. Luccock was saying, said with scorn, "Religion is a lot of moonshine."

Dr. Luccock thought a minute. Then he asked the student, "Have you ever seen a thirty-foot tide?" He went on to explain how the tide rolls in through the Bay of Fundy, on through Minas Basin, and on into Cobequid Bay. When the tide is out, the basin and the bay are nothing but mudflats too treacherous to venture out on. Ships have to be held upright by huge wooden cradles. Then the tide comes in and piles up to a depth of thirty feet or more, so that ships are free to sail out to the ports of the world.

"What makes the difference between the mudflats and the tide?" asked Dr. Luccock, and then he answered his own question by saying, "Moonshine." "For a tide," he went on to explain, "is caused by the pull of the moon on the earth. It is the pull of another world on this. And that essentially," he said, "is what religion is. It is the pull of another world on this. It is the pull of the world of the spirit on the world of the flesh. It is the pull of the life of God on the life of the world. It is the pull of the cross on our crassness."

A tide cannot create itself; its rise is a response to something. Our faith is also a response to something. We do not create our own faith. If we are Christians, it is a response to what God has done for us through Christ and his cross.

The world today is covered by treacherous mudflats of sin. We need to feel the tide of the Spirit that can enable us to sail in faith toward God and in love toward our neighbor, a tide that turns ugliness into beauty and lifts us into the freedom of God's love.

The Royal Mile

In the city of Edinburgh, Scotland, there is a street called the "Royal Mile." It runs from Edinburgh Castle to Holyroodhouse Palace, where Mary Queen of Scots lived for six years prior to her incarceration and subsequent execution.

The street runs past St. Giles Cathedral, where the ruling monarch of Britain worships when visiting Edinburgh, and continues on past the house where John Knox, the fiery defender of Protestantism, once lived, and on downhill to Holyroodhouse.

In the city of Jerusalem there is another street, called the Via Dolorosa. It is believed to be the street along which Jesus carried his cross on the way to his crucifixion.

The Royal Mile in Edinburgh reminds us of history. The Via Dolorosa in Jerusalem reminds us of God's greatest act of self-revelation in history. The Royal Mile reminds us of kings and queens. The Via Dolorosa reminds us of him who is the King of Kings. The Royal Mile dead-ends at Holyroodhouse Palace. The Via Dolorosa leads to a cross, but doesn't stop there. It leads on to a resurrection.

To walk the Royal Mile in Edinburgh is to be reminded of a queen who lost her life and her crown. To walk the Via Dolorosa in Jerusalem is to be reminded of him who gave his life to offer others an eternal crown. To walk toward Holyroodhouse is to go downhill. To walk toward the cross is to climb to new heights of spiritual peace and power.

3
The Miracle of the Resurrection

I once described to the late Dr. Halford Luccock something of my own religious pilgrimage. I grew up in a very conservative atmosphere. It never occurred to me to question anything in the Bible. Then, in school, I began to question many things in the Bible.

But one thing held me steady. That was the resurrection. I knew that if that were not true, the Bible is not "good news"; it is only advice for this life. We have only a king-size note of despair if everything ends at the grave. The more I have read the Bible, the more I have felt assured that something happened on that first Easter morning which convinced the disciples beyond a shadow of a doubt that Christ was risen from the dead. If I believed that, then I saw I was inconsistent to doubt the rest of what the Bible said about Jesus. So I worked my way back to an evangelical faith in the Bible.

Dr. Luccock listened patiently. Then he said, "You remind me of a young man who looked down into the Grand Canyon for the first time and said 'Something must have happened there.' "

Something did happen at the resurrection—something that changed the disciples from fearful followers into dauntless disciples. Something happened there that made Jesus the Savior of the world. Something happened there that gives us our greatest basis for believing in life after death. Something happened there that gives us our greatest incentive for noble living. If all human life ends at the grave, then our efforts to live for God are a mockery, and God is the chief mocker. But we are not animated rocks to be thrown into an abyss of nothingness at death. God has made us for eternity. Jesus' resurrection enables us to look beyond the grave and see the prospect of life with him stretching off into eternity.

We can never fully understand or grasp the mystery of what happened on that first Easter, but we thank God for the biblical witness that something wonderful that morning convinced his followers that Christ was indeed risen from the dead and lives today as our Savior. Many illustrations turn our attention to this glorious event.

You Better Believe It

It was Easter morning. I turned on the radio. A worship service was being broadcast from a church where the members respond audibly to the preacher's message. There were many "amens." Occasionally, someone would say, "That's right." Once when the minister declared in a loud voice, "Christ is risen from the dead," a voice from the congregation called out "You better believe it."

What an appropriate response to the message of the resurrection! Indeed, we *had* better believe it. For if Christ is not risen, then evil, not God, won the victory at Calvary. If Christ is not risen, how can he be our Savior? Or how can we believe in his promises? If Christ is not risen, we have no positive assurance of life after death. If Christ is not risen, we have lost our greatest basis for hope, and our greatest incentive for noble living.

"But in fact Christ has been raised from the dead" (1 Corinthians 15:20). The women discovered his rising. The disciples confirmed it. The apostles proclaimed it. The Bible records it. Christian experience affirms it. All of life takes on new meaning because of it. To believe in Christ's resurrection is a passport to fuller life here and to confidence in life beyond the grave.

Now we know that "eat, drink, and be merry, for tomorrow we die" is a lie. Tomorrow we live. We had better believe it. We dare not ignore the warnings of Scripture, or reject its invitation to faith.

Easter Sounds a Warning

Easter is not good news to everyone. It was not good news to the brilliant French writer Voltaire. Though Voltaire claimed to be a believer in God, he rejected the Christian idea of God and ridiculed the idea of life after death.

On his deathbed, however, he began to doubt his doubts. Suppose there were a heaven and a hell, after all. He knew in which one he deserved to spend eternity. And so, as almost his last utterance, he cried out, "I am abandoned by God and man! I shall go to hell! O Christ! O Jesus Christ!"

Whether God sensed any penitence in that cry, we do not know. We do know that Voltaire died in terror of what would lie ahead for one like himself who had ridiculed the goodness of God.

So, strange as it may seem, the message of Easter is not good news to everyone. It is not good news to those who live as if there were no God. It is not good news to those who live by the philosophy, "Eat, drink, and be merry, for tomorrow we die." If Easter is true, then tomorrow we live again! The question is no longer, "Is there life after death?" Jesus' resurrection has answered that one. The question is, "Where will we spend eternity?"

Many of us are concerned with what is happening in America. The rise in violence and crime! The resurgence of hate groups! The evidence of greed in our society! The widespread disrespect of law! The increasing use of drugs! The disregard for God and God's commandments!

There may be those who do not fear the courts of law, but they had better fear the court of heaven. The courts of human justice may not deter them, but they had better think twice about the court of God's judgment. The sentence handed down in that court is for eternity, and eternity is a long, long time.

Light on the Porch

Dr. Shields Hardin was an outstanding Baptist minister back in the days when bottled milk was delivered daily to people's homes. When his son was a small child, Shields asked him to put two empty milk bottles on the porch, so the milkman could pick them up early in the morning when he delivered new milk. The child took the bottles as far as the door, and then stopped. His father asked him, "Why don't you put the bottles on the porch?" The child turned and said, "It's too dark to go out there tonight without a father."

So Dr. Hardin walked out on the porch. The minute he was there, the child forgot all about the darkness. He ran out on the porch as if it were bright noon. His fear of the darkness was gone.

Notice that the boy's father gave him courage to walk *through* the door. Here is a parable of our Heavenly Father. The Psalmist says that at death we walk *through* the valley of the shadow of death. We don't stop in it. We go *through* it. Death is not a stopping-place. It is a passageway to a new and larger experience. We need not fear the darkness. God is there, and where God is, there is light.

When we face the last door, it means everything to know that Jesus himself went through that door and came back to tell us God was with him all the way. I once heard a minister say, "Jesus knocked both ends out of the tomb and made it a tunnel into eternity."

Sometimes the way ahead looks dark and foreboding, but God is standing by. When we see only the porch, we see darkness. But when we see the Father, we see light, for he *is* light.

Floors and Ceilings

I wish that this room had a floor;
I really don't care for a door;
But this walking around
With both feet off the ground,
Is getting to be such a bore.

Who wrote this silly little verse, I do not know. And yet there is a lot of sense in it. We don't want to float around in a meaningless sort of existence. We want to feel that life is upheld by a worthwhile meaning and purpose.

That's where faith in God comes in. It gives us a floor to live on. Life, the Bible tells us, is not just a meaningless void. It is based on the solid reality of God's existence and the assurance of God's love and purpose for our lives.

Moreover, through Christ, God gives us a floor of hope to live on. Jesus did not say, "In my Father's *houses* are many rooms." He said, "In my Father's *house* . . ." (John 14:2). To him, heaven and earth are so interrelated that they are only different rooms in the same house under the same overarching roof of God's love.

To die, then, can be likened to going upstairs to find rest and renewal in another room of the same house. What to us is a ceiling hiding those who have gone from this life is to them another floor on which they can live anew.

The Greatest Day of Your Life

Dr. Roy Burkhart was a gifted leader. He led the First Community Church of Columbus, Ohio, to become one of the truly great churches in America.

One day he returned to visit relatives in Pennsylvania. He was met in Harrisburg and taken to his home. As they crossed the Susquehanna river, the person who had come to meet him said, "I was baptized in that river forty years ago. That was the greatest day in my life." Dr. Burkhart said, "I'm sure it was a great day in your life. But do you want to know the greatest day in my life?" Naturally, the other person said, "Yes." Dr. Burkhart simply replied, "Tomorrow." In other words, however great his experience had been in the past, he was always looking forward to greater experience in the future.

Too many people, especially in religion, keep looking back. Many keep harking back to their conversion as if God had not spoken to them since that time. Of course, conversion is important, but it's only the beginning. God is not dead. The Holy Spirit is not idle. The Holy Spirit wants to lead us on to new heights of commitment and joy.

Of course, like the man who filled his barns (Luke 12:16-20), there comes to each of us a time when there is no tomorrow here on earth. But a Christian has a glorious hope. Even on the Christian's last day on earth, the affirmation still stands: "The greatest day of my life hasn't happened yet. It's tomorrow."

How can we know? How can we be sure? We know because Jesus tasted death and came back to reveal God's power over death. Thus Jesus has given us the confidence of an eternal tomorrow.

Belongings Above, Anyone?

In most modern jet passenger planes, there are compartments over the seats in which one can put a coat and hat and perhaps a small item of luggage. Often, as a plane begins its descent for landing, a flight attendant will go through the plane, take out the hats and coats, and hand them to their owners, so they will have them in hand when the plane lands.

On one plane the flight attendant asked the passengers, "Belongings above, anyone?" And if a passenger said yes, the attendant would hand the passenger his or her belongings.

In or out of a plane, this is a good question to ask: "Belongings above, anyone?"

It was Jesus himself who talked about the importance of having belongings above; that is, treasures in heaven (Matthew 6:19-20). Obviously, any attitude or act that would hurt another can never be a treasure in heaven. Only faith and love can be stored there.

The greatest treasure in heaven is one that God offers as a gift, and that is the divine love offered in Christ. Whoever receives that gift on earth can look forward to enjoying it in heaven.

Most of us are caught up in the effort to lay up treasures on earth. We must guard these against tarnish and thievery, but no one can steal our faith from us. God's love will never tarnish.

What is your answer to the question "Belongings above, anyone?"

Under Penalty of Death

The Church of the Epiphany is situated in the heart of downtown Washington, D. C., just three blocks east of the White House. It carries on a significant ministry in the downtown area of the nation's capital.

Some time ago, a member of the church staff with a delightful sense of humor taped a notice to the top of the pulpit. The notice said, "This prayer book must not be removed from this pulpit under penalty of death."

This warning given in jest reminds us of the first time a similar warning was ever issued—only then it was not a laughing matter. It was in the Garden of Eden. Our first parents were told not to eat of the forbidden tree under penalty of death (Genesis 3:3), but they were tempted to ignore the warning.

If only they had known! They did not have to eat of the forbidden fruit to enjoy themselves. There was so much in the garden for them to explore and enjoy—enough to satisfy them a thousand times over—but they set their hearts on the one thing they were told they should not have.

If they had known they were going to be put out of the garden, they might have had second thoughts. They might have thought of flowers they would never see again or of the fruit that was there for the taking. But they gave it all up by their self-indulgence and paid the price for their willfulness by having to accept back-breaking toil in a world outside the garden.

Paul reminds us that sin has brought all of us under the penalty of death (Romans 5:12). Our hope, however, is not in the Garden of Eden, where sin entered the world, but in the garden of the resurrection where the assurance of eternal life entered the world (John 19:41). Knowing that we will not live forever in this world should make us cherish each day as a wonderful gift from God. Even more than that, it should make us turn to Christ, who can change the penalty of death into the promise of eternal life.

Stradivarius Violin or
Cheap Fiddle?

One of the delights of music lovers in the nation's capital is the concerts of classical music by soloists and small groups held in the Library of Congress. For many years these featured the Budapest String Quartet and later the Juilliard String Quartet. In these concerts skilled musicians played on priceless Stradivarius instruments which did not belong to them but were the property of the Library of Congress. When the concerts were over, the musicians returned the instruments to the custodian, who kept them in a special place at the right temperature and humidity to preserve their resonance for centuries to come.

Our lives are like that. They are not ours to do with as we please. They come from God. They belong to God. One day they must be returned to God, who alone can keep them for eternity.

Yet some people treat their lives as if they were only cheap fiddles to be discarded when the concert season is over. Stradivarius would not have taken such pains to produce matchless instruments if he had expected them to be thrown away after the concert. And God would hardly have created each of us with a distinct and unique personality, if God intended us to be discarded forever at death.

In fact, the Bible says that this life is not the real concert. Life is only the rehearsal, where we get ourselves in tune with God's love and will and where we learn to play in harmony with others. As the instruments must be tuned to the piano's "A," so we must get in tune with God, who has sounded his "A" in the life and death of Christ. If we have not had practice in learning to live in harmony with others, how can we expect to be happy in heaven where everything is motivated by love?

From Puddles to Clouds

One day after a heavy rain, I noticed a large muddy puddle of water by the roadside. Children were wading in it. Perhaps it was the children that made me notice it.

Sometime later I went by the spot again. The children were gone, but the water was still there. Much of the silt had sunk to the bottom. The surface of the water had become a mirror reflecting the trees and the sky.

I thought how like life that is. All of us are conscious of the silt of sinful desires that muddies our lives. Sometimes we let the world roil it up. But, when we become quiet before God, the silt drops away, and we can reflect something of God's divine nature.

Still later, I went by the same place again. The water was gone. It had evaporated leaving the silt behind to show where the water had been. Then I looked up, and directly over where the puddle had been, there was a beautiful white cloud. It was almost as if the water from that puddle had gone to make that particular cloud. I felt like saying, "There's your puddle."

Someday people will say of us, "They're gone." But that won't be the end of us any more than evaporation brings an end to the water. The water does not cease to be when it vanishes from our sight. It is transformed into another form from which God can make a beautiful cloud.

So, faith leads us to believe, it will be with us at death. The silt of the flesh will be left behind. But the soul, the self, will be released to be clothed in what Paul called a spiritual body in which we can experience all the freedom and joy of heaven (1 Corinthians 15:44, 49).

Not Alone

My wife and I enjoy our home. In it we have furnishings and treasures we have accumulated through the years. Yet these things are only incidental to our happiness. We realize this truth especially when one of us is away and the other is there alone. The furnishings and the treasures are still there, but without the other person's presence the house seems empty. When both are there, even though we may be in different rooms, just knowing that the other is there makes all the difference in the world.

Believing that God is here in our lives—that there is no place where God is not—makes all the difference in how we look at life. But it is not enough just to believe in God's presence. It is not just my wife's presence that turns our house into a home. It is knowing she loves me that does that. And knowing not only that God is present, but that God loves us and sent Jesus to be our Redeemer, can make all the difference in how we look at life and death.

When the day comes that one of us is left alone on earth while the other one goes on ahead to the heavenly home, the one who is left behind will still have the promise of eternal life—a promise that became a "living hope" by Jesus' resurrection from the dead (1 Peter 1:3).

Two Octogenarians Speak

A millionaire octogenarian was talking to a friend of mine. To my friend, he said, "I'm an old man. I'm 80 years of age." And then, almost to himself, he added, "Here I am a millionaire, and I have to die."

Evidently, he brooded about his mortality. His enjoyment of his last years was clouded by the thought that death would rob him of all he had accumulated.

Another octogenarian was Annie Sherwood Hawks, who wrote the familiar hymn "I Need Thee Every Hour." In her eighty-first year she wrote to a young cousin, "There has no experience ever come to me, through all the years, more satisfying than that coming to me since I entered upon the probably last decade of my life here."

What a difference! Here were two people looking at life from the vantage point of the same age. One was worrying about the encroachment of death. The other was still savoring life. The one was made poorer by apprehensions about the end. The other was made richer because of a desire to live hourly closer to her Lord.

Death waits for all of us, but we don't have to be morbid about it. If our trust is in God, each day can be a wonderful new gift. Each decade can be richer because we bring to it a greater wealth of experience and understanding.

As we grow older, we tend to lose some of the impatience of youth and to gain a perspective that comes only through greater experience. We learn to accept our limitations with more grace and to be grateful for the wealth of experience we bring to each new day. And when death does come, if we have walked with the Lord, we can accept continuing life with God as the greatest gift of all.

4

The Need for Inner Renewal

Today's English Version translates Paul's words in Romans 12:2 this way: "Do not conform yourselves to the standards of this world, but let God transform you *inwardly* by a complete change of your mind." Or as J. B. Phillips translates it, "Don't let the world around you squeeze you into its own mould, but let God *re-mould* your minds from within."

That is where the Christian life begins. It begins within us. We are told to let our light shine out to others (Matthew 5:16), but how can it shine if there is no light? That's where the light must shine first—in our hearts. As the author of Proverbs put it, as a person thinks "in his heart," so is that person (Proverbs 23:7, KJV).

Jesus put it another way. "Are grapes gathered from thorns, or figs from thistles? So every sound tree bears good fruit, but the bad tree bears evil fruit" (Matthew 7:16-17). Or again, "If your eye is not sound, your whole body will be full of darkness. If then the light in you is darkness, how great is the darkness!" (Matthew 6:23).

That is where transformation must take place—within the heart and mind of the individual. That is where God speaks directly to the human soul. That is where we must say yes to God.

Someone has put it rather crudely, "No rearrangement of bad eggs can ever make a good omelet." There is no way that we can make a bad egg fresh again, but, when it comes to people, Christ can turn a bad person into a good person, a bad thought into a good thought, a bad attitude into a good attitude.

Fortunately, too, we are not alone in the struggle to find God and be found by God. The Holy Spirit directs our search and gives us the victory. The Spirit opens our eyes. As Jesus explained to Simon Peter, flesh and blood do not reveal the deep things of the Spirit. Only God can do that through the work of the Holy Spirit. It is the Spirit who opens our eyes to truths to which the world is blind.

The following illustrations point to the need for inner renewal and remind us that the Holy Spirit makes that renewal possible.

From Tedious Crawling to Triumphant Flying

One of the cleverest Mother's Day cards I have ever seen shows a picture of a caterpillar crawling along one end of a branch, while poised on the other end is a gorgeous butterfly. The caterpillar is saying to the butterfly, "Mother, you're beautiful."

How little the caterpillar realizes that in God's plan for its life there is the latent possibility of a similar transformation; that by surrendering its worm-likeness to the protective embrace of a silken cocoon, it too can emerge as a glorious creature of beauty and flight.

There is a similar possibility in each of us. Earthbound though we are, we can be born again into spiritual beauty and freedom. As the Bible puts it, we can "put on" Christ, so that the ugliness of our sin is taken away, and people can begin to see something of the beauty of Jesus in us (Ephesians 4:22-24).

This possibility helps us to love others in a new way. A caterpillar wantonly destroys the foliage on which it feeds, but a butterfly in no way harms the flowers from which it draws its sustenance. On the contrary, it carries pollen from flower to flower and so contributes to new growth and beauty. Many people feed their desires and ambitions at the expense of others. A sincere Christian, on the other hand, not only seeks to receive God's love but also tries to carry some of that love to other persons. Thus the Christian contributes to greater happiness in the world.

Finally, we have the promise that one day we will exchange our "physical body" for a "spiritual body." We will find that heavenly existence is more wonderful than earth—just as a butterfly that can fly in God's open air is more wonderful than a caterpillar that can only crawl on or near the earth (1 Corinthians 15:44, 49).

The Best Time to Plant the Potatoes

A wife wrote to her husband who was in prison for armed robbery, asking him, "When is the best time to plant the potatoes?" He wrote back, "Don't dig in the garden. That's where I hid my guns."

All the mail going in and out of the prison was censored, and when the guards read that sentence, they sent out a group of men who dug up the garden from one end to the other, but didn't find a gun. When the wife reported what they had done, her husband replied, "The garden is ready. Now is the time to plant the potatoes."

Seed cannot be planted in hard ground. The ground must be spaded or plowed. The earth must be broken up so that the seed can be inserted in the soil, and so that water can penetrate to the seed and later to the roots.

Hard hearts need to be broken up, too. Hard, resistant pride needs to be cracked open so the healing, transforming love of God can penetrate. A life must feel the penetrating blade of the Spirit and the cutting edge of repentance before faith can grow. The hard-caked crust of self-sufficiency must be turned over. The sun-baked love of sin must be turned under. The moist loam of discipleship must be brought to the surface to receive the seed of God's purpose and will.

The showers of God's love will run off the hardened surface of an unloving life. Faith cannot grow there. Only the weeds of selfishness and cynicism can grow in such a soil.

Like birds that follow the plow, so peace and joy will follow in the furrows of a life that is upturned to God. A broken and a contrite heart is the sign of a good harvest to come. That harvest includes all the promises of God.

But we cannot prepare the garden alone. We are not strong enough to push a plow. Something has to pull it. We must be willing to let the transforming power of God's love pull our stubborn wills toward repentance and faith.

Jet Planes and White Orchids

It was Sunday morning in the First Baptist Church of Minneapolis. The organist had come to the end of the prelude. The pastor, Peter West, had seated himself on the pulpit platform. Suddenly over the public address system there came the sound of a jet plane rising into the sky. People looked at each other in surprise—and yet not total surprise. What was the pastor up to this time?

The sound of the plane faded away. Quietly the pastor rose and began to recite verses from the Psalm 139: "Whither shall I go from thy Spirit? Or whither shall I flee from thy presence? . . . If I take the wings of the morning and dwell in the uttermost parts of the sea, even there thy hand shall lead me, and thy right hand shall hold me."

The chances are the worshipers never forgot that call to worship. Moreover, it made it easy for them to witness. They probably rushed out to tell others, "Guess what happened in our church this morning!"

Another time the pastor entered the pulpit and held up a pure white orchid. He told how the tuber for this flower had once been covered by muck in a flood. But the owner had cleansed it, and tenderly cared for it, and after seven years of patiently waiting, this beautiful blossom had appeared.

Again he made it easy for them to witness. Again worshipers could go out to tell their friends, "Guess how our pastor started the service this morning!"

In these days when it is literally possible to take the wings of the morning and fly to the uttermost parts of the sea, where do we look for God? Look beyond the farthest star and God is there. Look in the workings of history and God is there. Look within the human heart and God is there waiting to be recognized.

And what is God doing? God is trying to cleanse us from the muck of sin, trying patiently to bring out the beauty of character that is there, because it was for this God created us.

Just Tulips or Cups of Light?

They were beautiful tulips. Could I capture their beauty on film so I could enjoy it all through the year? I noticed that the background was in the shadow, and that the sun was shining on the tulips, so I knelt down and took a picture of the flowers.

The result was more spectacular than I had expected. When I took the picture, the sun was shining at just the right angle to fill the tulips with light. It was as if each tulip had a light glowing inside it. As a result the tulips were turned into cups of light.

Any photographer knows the supreme importance of lighting in taking a picture. The object being photographed may be beautiful, the camera a good one, the film sensitive, but the result will be disappointing if the light is not right. It is lighting that makes the picture. It can turn an otherwise ordinary picture into a great one.

So it is with life. The light of God can shine on an ordinary life and make it luminous with faith. God is light (1 John 1:5). God lets the light shine on all people. Persons who receive that light and let it shine from within reveal its true beauty.

True beauty comes from within. Cosmetics cannot compete with character. Beauty of face can fade with age, but beauty of character can increase as one grows older, especially when it glows with compassion and concern for others. When the beauty of character is touched by the light of a deep faith in God, the result can be beautiful indeed. And the best way to let the beauty of God be upon us is to learn of Jesus in whom the light of divine love shone perfectly. Even the darkness of Calvary could not put it out.

A Glimpse of God's Truth in Us

Jimmy Owens has written a song entitled "Forgive Me, My Friend," in which he turns the picture of Christian witness around. Instead of urging us to look for glimpses of God's truth outside ourselves, he asks if we are failing those who look to see a glimpse of Christ in us.

A glimpse of Christ in us! Peter and John showed the Jewish leaders a glimpse of Christ's courage in them when they refused to stop preaching in his name (Acts 4:18-19). Stephen showed his murderers a glimpse of Christ's forgiving love in him when he prayed for the people who were stoning him (Acts 7:60). Paul showed the world many a glimpse of Christ's presence in him by the way he bore his persecutions. Most Christians are led to faith in Christ by the glimpses of Christ they have seen in the lives of Christians who have influenced them.

Jimmy Owens's song raises many questions. Has anyone been led closer to Christ by a glimpse of Christ he has seen in us? Has our resistance to temptation reminded others of Christ's victory over sin? Has our trust in Christ shown through in the way we have borne our griefs, faced our disappointments, treated those who have mistreated us? Have we failed others who may have looked for a glimpse of Christ in us?

What's Eating You?

In his book *The Medusa and the Snail* Dr. Lewis Thomas, noted pathologist, describes an interesting happening in nature. The medusa is a jellyfish. The snail belongs to the nudibranch variety. Both live in the Bay of Naples.

Sometimes, when a snail is small, a jellyfish will swallow it by drawing it into its digestive tract. But the snail is protected by its shell and cannot be digested. So it, in turn, fastens itself to the jellyfish and begins to eat the jellyfish. By the time the snail is fully grown, it has entirely consumed the jellyfish that swallowed it in the first place. One is reminded of Paul's warning, "But if you bite and devour one another, take heed that you are not consumed by one another" (Galatians 5:15).

The moral of Dr. Thomas's book could well be "be careful what you swallow." Or a good subtitle could be "What's eating you?"— which is a good question to ask. For some it is alcoholism that eats them from within. They take an occasional drink. But gradually the desire for alcohol begins to gnaw at them, and they end up being consumed by a thirst they cannot control.

For others it may be resentment. Someone does a hateful thing to us, so we hate them back. We hang on to our resentment until we end up being consumed by it. Or it may be worry. Something sets us off, and we begin to worry about it until we can hardly think of anything else.

It may be greed that eats us. A merchant tries to increase his profits by selling inferior merchandise at excessively high prices, and in time his business collapses.

It hardly needs to be said that any sin is like these. We commit a sin, and it seems easy. The desire to commit it again begins to gnaw at us. Unless we resist it and turn to God for help, we may end up being consumed by an evil passion we cannot control.

Stars in Cherry Blossoms

Early spring in Washington, D. C., means Japanese cherry blossoms. Thousands of people pour into the city each year to see the famous blossoms around the Tidal Basin near downtown Washington. Others go to an area called Kenwood in nearby Bethesda, Maryland, to see a fairyland of blossom-laden trees lining both sides of the streets for several blocks.

Most people look at the blossoms without ever seeing an interesting detail. In the center of every Japanese cherry blossom there is a perfect star. It is small, but it is there. Once you have noticed this detail, you can never look at Japanese cherry blossoms again without seeing the stars at the center.

One wonders what God sees when looking at the center of our lives. A dollar sign? A sex symbol? A social ladder? A workbench or desk? Compassion for others? Commitment to God?

That's where God looks—at the center. Samuel found that out. Saul was taller and more handsome than all the other young men in Kish (1 Samuel 9:2). He would be an impressive-looking king. So Samuel chose him to be the first king of Israel. It was a poor decision, because there was seething jealousy at the center of Saul's life, and he proved to be something less than a great king.

So Samuel had to look for another. This time he was impressed by Eliab's appearance, but God warned him not to make the same mistake twice. "Man looks on the outward appearance, but the Lord looks on the heart" (1 Samuel 16:7). So Samuel chose David, who proved himself worthy by having "more success than all the servants of Saul" (1 Samuel 18:30).

By magnifying a picture of a cherry blossom, the star at the center becomes very apparent. If Christ is at the center of our lives, the more we magnify him, the more beautiful we are in the sight of God.

The First Hundred Days

When a president of the United States has been in office for one hundred days, a number of articles appear in the newspapers and magazines evaluating his effectiveness during that period. Evidently, editors and commentators feel that he has been in office long enough by then to establish certain trends in dealing with national and international problems.

What about the most recent hundred days of our lives? What have they revealed about us? Is anyone happier because we lived them? Is God any more conscious of our love? Have we added to our knowledge?

When William H. Danforth was a boy, he tended to be underweight and sickly. One day, one of his teachers who was a health enthusiast, said to him, "William, I dare you to become the healthiest person in this class." Young Danforth accepted the challenge, and by wise eating habits and plenty of outdoor exercise he built a body that served him well when he became the president of the Ralston-Purina Food Mills.

In later years, he published a small book entitled *I Dare You,* in which he challenged his reader to know more about some worthwhile subject than anyone else in the community. In some communities that would be a tall order. But if you are willing to put forth the effort, you can become an authority on some worthwhile subject of your choosing.

God willing, another hundred days are ahead of each of us. Will they be any different from the last hundred, or just the same? How can we use them for personal growth? How can we serve God and our neighbors better?

Why not set some goals for ourselves, and mark a day on the calendar one hundred days from now? When that day comes, we can check ourselves to see what we have accomplished.

5

The Ministry of the Holy Spirit

Dr. H. Wheeler Robinson tells us that once, when he was critically ill, he was disturbed to find that the Christian truths he declared so confidently to others were not seeming to give him the support he thought they would in a time of severe crisis. Perhaps it was because he was so sick. The body can affect the mind just as the mind can affect the body.

He decided that one of the reasons he felt this way was that he had not thought enough about the presence of the Holy Spirit in his life. So, when he recovered, he set himself to the task of studying everything the Bible has to say about the Holy Spirit. The result was that fifteen years later, he published his great book entitled *The Christian Experience of the Holy Spirit.*

One wonders if many Christians do not have a similar problem. They believe in the truth of the gospel but for some reason do not feel the thrill of it. They believe in the validity of the Christian message but do not seem to feel its vitality. Perhaps they, too, need to think more about Jesus' promise of the Holy Spirit; about the reality and presence of the Holy Spirit in their lives.

I once faced this same problem. I was a Christian clergyman. I loved Jesus and I knew he loved me, but I felt a dryness in my life. So I asked God for two things. I asked God to take out of my life everything that was keeping me from being the kind of person God wanted me to be. And I asked God to fill me with his Spirit.

I don't know what I expected to happen. I didn't see any visions. I didn't talk in tongues. But I did begin to feel a new sense of God's presence. I no longer prayed to a God "out there," but to one who was very much with me in the person of the Holy Spirit. I felt a new urgency to seek God's guidance daily——to be submissive to God's leading. My greatest moments in the ministry have not been those when I felt I shone because of my abilities, but when I felt most conscious of being blessed and used by the Holy Spirit.

These illustrations stress the ministry of the Holy Spirit.

Hands Off the Spirit

In his excellent book *Rapping About the Spirit,* Dr. Bernard Ramm warns against the danger of elevating the importance of an inner, subjective experience of the Holy Spirit so much that it obscures the objective revelation of God's purpose and will in Jesus Christ. After all, the Holy Spirit was not sent to take the place of Christ, but to exalt him and interpret him, so as to help us better understand and follow his call (John 14:26).

Yet having said this, Dr. Ramm goes on to add that "if the charismatic movement tells us anything, it tells us that people are hungering for more than the church is giving them."

Part of this hunger may be due to the strange silence concerning the presence and ministry of the Holy Spirit to be found in most of the churches. Oh yes, they mention the Holy Spirit from time to time, but they hardly seek to make people fully aware of the Spirit's presence and power.

When the world would no longer have his physical presence, Jesus promised the presence of the Comforter or Counselor (John 14:16), the word so translated meaning "one who is called alongside."

Of this One, Jesus said the world could neither see nor receive him (John 14:17). The word translated "receive" can also mean "to lay hold of with one's hand." Some Bible scholars have pointed out that, soon after these words were spoken, the soldiers would lay hands on Jesus. They would arrest him and take him away. But the world can never lay its hands on the Holy Spirit or take the Spirit away from us, because the Spirit is not physical. The world does not even know the Spirit exists, but—if we seek, through Bible study, prayer, and fellowship with other dynamic Christians—we can sense the Spirit's presence.

Circles on a Ceiling

Dr. Dale Moody, of Southern Baptist Seminary in Louisville, told me of an ancient church that had three circles, one inside the other, painted on the ceiling directly over the baptistry. The circles, of course, represented the Trinity. I said, "The outside circle must represent God the Father, being all-inclusive." "No," he replied, "the outer circle represents the Holy Spirit. You have to go through that circle to get to the next circle representing Christ, just as you have to go through that circle to get to the inner circle representing God, the Father, who is the heart of it all."

In other words, it is the Holy Spirit who opens our eyes to see the lordship of Christ, just as it is through Christ we know the redeeming love of God.

Long before the Trinity was a doctrine, it was an experience. The followers of Jesus believed in God before they knew Jesus. They knew God through the law and the prophets. But then they met Jesus. They had never seen anyone like him. He didn't just *talk* about love; he *loved* them. He didn't just talk about sacrifice. He went to the cross. He didn't just talk about life after death. He rose from the dead. They could believe him when he said, "I and the Father are one" (John 10:30).

At Pentecost they had a new experience. Surely this was the power of the Holy Spirit Jesus had promised them. With this power, they were made bold to run out and tell the world that Jesus is Christ and Lord.

This same Holy Spirit is with us today. The Spirit can help us to know Christ as our personal Lord and Savior. The Spirit helps us to know the mind of Christ for our lives and for the world today. And, insofar as we exalt Christ and his way of life, we do honor to God the Creator.

The Other Helper

Water is one of the most important elements in the world. Without water all life on this planet would cease to exist. In many parts of the world water is more precious than diamonds. People can live without diamonds, but they cannot live without water.

Water exists in three forms, and in each of these it does something for us that it does not do in the other forms. As liquid, it quenches our thirst. As vapor, or steam, it warms our houses. In solid form, or ice, it preserves our food. But it is all water.

So it is with God. God the Father creates us. God the Son redeems us. God the Holy Spirit guides and sustains us. But it is all God.

In his book *Spirit, Son and Father,* Dr. Henry P. Van Dusen says that in God the Father we see the *ultimacy* of God; in God the Son we see the *character* of God; and in God the Holy Spirit we experience the *intimacy* of God.

It was this intimacy, this nearness of God, that Jesus had in mind when he said he would send "another" Comforter, or Helper. Here it helps us to know a little Greek. When Paul said that if even an angel from heaven were to preach *another* gospel than the one he proclaimed, he should be accursed (Galatians 1:8, KJV), he used the word "heteron," which means *another of a different kind.* But when John recorded Jesus' words, he used the word "alle," which means *another of the same kind* (John 14:16). In other words, the Holy Spirit is the Spirit of Christ ministering to us without Christ's physical presence.

The world cannot take the Holy Spirit from us. The world doesn't even know the Spirit exists. Nevertheless, through the work of the Holy Spirit, Christ can enter our hearts.

Have You Done Your Homework?

A certain person was invited to address a meeting of Christian young people. When he was presented, he stood and after an awkward silence he said, "I always depend on the Holy Spirit to tell me what to say. He has not told me tonight, so I have no message for you." Then he sat down.

There was a stunned silence. The leader suggested they sing some hymns. After the "speaker" had left, the young people remained behind. Who had failed, they wanted to know, the Holy Spirit or the speaker? Unanimously, they agreed it was the person who had been invited to speak. One person tried to come to his defense. Did not Jesus promise that the Holy Spirit would tell us what to say? Others pointed out that this promise was for those who are tested and persecuted for their faith (Matthew 10:16-19).

There is a wonderful word in the King James Version of the New Testament. It is the word "quicken." We find it in John 6:63, Romans 8:11, Ephesians 2:1, 1 Peter 3:18, and elsewhere. The Holy Spirit can quicken us, but we must provide something to be quickened. The Spirit can quicken our understanding of the Bible, but only if we read the Bible. The Spirit can quicken our prayer life, but only if we pray. The Spirit can quicken our influence, but only if we live a life of love and service. The Spirit can quicken our spiritual perceptions, but only if we commit our lives to Christ. The Spirit can help us pass the tests of life, but we must do our homework. We must offer something to be quickened.

We must not expect the Holy Spirit to do our work for us. God wants willing hands as well as surrendered hearts. But we must have God's help. We can bear a witness, but only the Holy Spirit can convict and convert. We can speak a word of comfort, but only the Spirit can give a peace that passes understanding. They go together: our preparation and God's power, our labor and God's love.

On Being a Straight Arrow

During the Korean war I went to speak to American troops stationed on several islands in the Pacific, as well as Japan and Korea itself. I used to watch the men as they went off the bases on leave. They didn't have to go looking for temptation. Temptation came looking for them. Young women, many of them attractive, were waiting to be picked up by the soldiers. Many were ready to "shack up" with the Americans, that is, live with them while they were in the area, in return for the standard of living the Americans could provide for them.

The temptation for our troops was tremendous. They were away from home. They were lonely. They felt lost in a strange land. They craved affection. Many of them fell for the temptation that was so obvious. They were often referred to as broken arrows.

But some did not fall. They were known as straight arrows. Some of them were even given small straight arrows as emblems to carry with them as reminders to live a clean life.

Why were some men able to resist the temptation when others fell? Many, I am sure, resisted because they thought of someone back home, a wife or mother or sweetheart, someone who would be grievously hurt if they knew that their loved one had crossed the Pacific to win a war, and had lost the battle against temptation. Others, I am also sure, resisted because they knew there was Someone closer than a wife or mother or sweetheart who was with them at all times, and who would be deeply grieved if they lost the battle with sin.

That Someone, of course, was God's Holy Spirit. That Spirit is with us at all times to strengthen us, and is deeply grieved when we fall. That is why Paul put it so bluntly. In Ephesians 4:30 he wrote, "Do not grieve the Holy Spirit of God."

Grass Among the Rocks

There is a legend in the Middle East that, when creating the world, God filled two bags full of rocks and asked two angels to scatter them over the face of the earth. One angel flew off to carry out God's bidding, but the other got over Judea and the bag broke.

We need to remember that the promise "He maketh me to lie down in green pastures" was not written in Oklahoma where "the corn is as high as an elephant's eye." It was written in Palestine, where there are some of the most barren and rocky areas to be found anywhere on the face of the earth. The shepherd must not only know about sheep. He must know how to find grass and water for his sheep.

Many persons have discovered that it is precisely in rocky circumstances that God's presence is most revealed to them. Dr. William Axling discovered this fact during a war. He was a missionary to Japan. When war broke out between Japan and the United States in 1941, he and his wife were held under house arrest in Tokyo for a year. As the war continued, they were separated and taken to different concentration camps. Dr. Axling asked for permission to take his Bible with him, but his request was denied.

First his freedom was taken away. Then his wife was taken away. Then his Bible was denied him. But his captors could not take the Holy Spirit from him. They did not even know the Holy Spirit exists. Yet Dr. Axling said that God was never more real to him than in those days when he shivered in an unheated cell, and had to commit his wife and his friends to the watchcare of God. In the midst of such a barren experience, God helped him to find green pastures of the soul.

6

Commitment and Trust

In his book *The Life of the Soul,* the late Samuel Miller, who served as pastor of the First Baptist Church of Cambridge, Mass., and chaplain of the Harvard Divinity School, wrote: "We have come to feel very tolerant and comfortable, as though every soul, regardless of its self-neglect or self-destructiveness, will come at last to have heaven dropped into its undeserving hands. This belief is not in the New Testament."

One cannot crash the gates of heaven. One must accept God's invitation on God's terms. One does not drift into the Christian life. The Christian life calls for decision and commitment. One must decide whether to be a Christian. One may decide yes or no, for or against—one has that choice, and to ignore it or put it off is to make a negative decision. Having made it, however, one must live with the consequences of that choice.

Jesus never said it would be easy to follow him. On the contrary, he was constantly telling his followers how hard it would be. Some went away sorrowfully because they could not measure up to his demands (Matthew 19:22). But for those who remained steadfast, even though they had moments of failure, he opened up a whole new life and venture for them.

The call to decision and commitment comes today. For those who live in an anti-Christian culture, the cost is apt to be exceedingly high. For all it means sincere repentance—a complete break with a sinful and indifferent past—and a total commitment to the way of Christ.

The following illustrations and their brief messages focus attention on the need to make such a serious and important commitment.

All or Nothing

In many Baptist churches an invitation to Christian discipleship is given at each service. Those desiring to profess personal faith in Christ, or to transfer their church membership, are invited to indicate their decision by coming forward during the singing of an "invitation hymn." Those who respond are sometimes asked, "How do you come?" meaning, "Do you come to profess faith in Christ, or to request membership by a transfer of your church letter?"

Sometimes the question gets an unexpected answer. In response to the question, "How do you come?" one woman answered, "By bus."

But the best of all answers to this question was given to the Rev. Charles Nunn when he was the pastor of the First Baptist Church of Bluefield, West Virginia. In response to the question, "How do you come" one person replied, "Without reservations."

That is how God wants us all to come—without reservations. But it is so easy to come *with* reservations, giving God only part of our lives. It is easy to invite God into our prayers, but not our pleasures; into our worship, but not our work. It is easy to offer God all the keys to our life but one. We say, "Please let me keep the key to this one area for myself." But God says, "No, it won't work. All the time you'd be thinking about that one area, and so would I. Give me the key to *every* room in your life, and I will flood *every* corner with my peace and joy."

Many a person has thought that happiness depended on freedom to continue in some particular sin—only to discover, upon surrendering that sin to God, what real happiness is. The joy that is known then is not clouded with self-reproach or fear of being found out; it's a joy that can come only in giving oneself to God "without reservations."

The Grip of the Father's Hand

One of the most pleasant sensations we can experience in this world is the feel of a small child's hand in ours as the child walks along beside us. The softness and warmth of that touch, speaking as they do of the child's trust in us and dependence upon us, go directly to an older person's heart.

I once passed a father leading his small daughter by the hand. He smiled down to her as she talked excitedly up to him. She fairly danced as she skipped along at his side. I saw them only in passing, but the sight of them made my day. Every time I remember it, it warms my heart.

There is added joy in heaven, Jesus said, when we let go of sin and reach up to take hold of God's hand (Luke 15:10).

But, as anyone who has ever tried to lead a small child by the hand knows, often the child will try to pull its hand away. It considers the grip of the older person's hand too much of a restraint on its desire to be free. It wants to exercise its independence even at the risk of a danger the child is neither old enough nor experienced enough to understand.

It's the same problem with God's children. They tug and pull to be free, and then blame God for not giving them greater protection when they run into trouble.

A religious song urges us to put our hand in the hand of the Man of Galilee. That is one security life cannot take from us. That is why Louise Haskins wrote, "Put your hand in the hand of God. That shall be to you better than light, and safer than a known way."

Stand Up and Stand Out

There is a story about a man who was passionately fond of yellow. In his room the walls and ceiling were painted yellow. There was a yellow wall-to-wall carpet. The draperies, the bedspread, even his pajamas were yellow.

And then one day the poor man got yellow jaundice.

His wife sent for the doctor and waited outside the room until the doctor had examined her husband. In a moment, the doctor came out looking puzzled. "How is he?" asked the wife. "I don't know," replied the doctor. "I can't find him."

Often there is so little difference between those who call themselves "Christians" and those who do not that one can hardly tell them apart. Many Christians merge so completely into their secular background that they do not stand out in any way. Gordon Cosby, founder of the Church of the Savior in Washington, D. C., states the problem this way: "We try to send into the world healers who have not themselves been healed. We want our congregations to be reconcilers who have not themselves been reconciled. We would have them proclaim the word when they have heard no word to proclaim."

This was not true of the first Christians. They stood out from the world in which they lived. They stood out in their dependence on prayer. They stood out in the boldness with which many of them proclaimed their faith. They stood out in such sharp contrast to some of the accepted customs and beliefs of their day that some of them were actually called "these men who have turned the world upside down" (Acts 17:6).

Christians today are called upon to stand up and stand out. They are called to stand up for their convictions concerning God's will for the world. They are called to stand out in courageous and yet loving ways as they try to influence their world.

A Definition of Faith

I once made a collection of unusual definitions. One that I liked was Dr. Bernard Clausen's definition of a pearl. "A pearl," he said, "is a garment of patience wrapped around an annoyance." But one of my favorites was Dr. Kirsopp Lake's definition of faith. "Faith," he said, "is not belief in spite of evidence, but life in scorn of consequence." Dr. Elton Trueblood later simplified this definition by saying, "Faith is not belief without proof, but trust without reservations."

Faith is more than belief. Faith is belief expressed in action. I may believe that it is safe to fly, and yet never set foot inside an airplane. I demonstrate my faith in flying only when I board the plane and fasten my seat belt. I may believe certain things *about* God, and yet never surrender my life to God. After all, even devils "believe—and shudder" (James 2:19), but they don't repent. I demonstrate my faith when I surrender my life to God and try to live by God's will.

Faith is not just sitting around waiting for God to do something. Faith is launching out where we believe God is leading; it is believing that if we trust completely, God will guide and support us all the way.

So it was with the children of Israel. Caught between Pharaoh's army and the Red Sea, they panicked. Moses tried to calm their fears. "Stand firm," he said, "and see the salvation of the Lord, which he will work for you today." But God didn't like that advice. "Tell the people of Israel to go forward," he said (Exodus 14:13-15). When they demonstrated their faith by going forward, God's plan for their liberation was revealed to them.

A Decision's Distance

Since my cottage in Maine sits on the top of a ridge, there is a forty- or fifty-mile view from both the front and the back of the cottage. The more spectacular view, however, is to be seen from the rear of the cottage.

A certain woman of the area came to visit us. As she stepped from her car, she said, "My, you have a lovely view here." I replied, "You haven't seen anything yet." I led her around behind the cottage. When she reached the point where she could see parts of two lakes and a range of the White Mountains in the distance, she said, "I have lived within twenty miles of this view all my life, and never knew it was here."

Later I shared her comment with a group and added, "Millions of people live within a decision's distance of all the joys and rewards of the Christian life and do not know they are there, because they refuse to go around behind whatever is blocking them from God."

Some people fail to experience the peace and joy of the Christian life because they think Christians don't have any fun. To be sure, some Christians do give that impression, but a true Christian has found a way of life that is exciting and rewarding, and that gives a joy that lasts.

A young man once told Dr. Roy Burkhart that he was an atheist, but he was intrigued by some of the young people who came to Dr. Burkhart's church. They seemed to be so alive, and had so much fun. Dr. Burkhart challenged the youth to meet with the group, and to begin living as if he did believe in God and wanted to please God. In time, the youth was led to become a Christian because, as he put it, he had discovered "it's more fun being a Christian than it is going to the devil."

What Do You Want?

A little boy came home from Sunday School and announced that he had learned a new Bible verse. When asked what it was, he said, "The Lord is my shepherd, that's all I want."

That's not a bad way to say it. Unfortunately, we live in a world that encourages us to want much more. Sometimes when a child asks for something, the child's mother will say, "Your wants are never satisfied." Advertisers would like to keep it that way.

As a result, we want far more than we need. If our neighbor has something new, we want it too. If it's a new model, we want it. If we think it's a bargain, we want it. Sometimes just because it is advertised, we want it.

We need to check our wants against our needs. Of course, we need food, clothing, and lodging. Jesus said that God knows we have need of these things (Matthew 6:32). We need friendship, acceptance, hope, and love. We need to feel a sense of fulfillment. If we have these, though, it is surprising how many other things we can get along without.

Above all, we need faith in God. This is a need some people don't seem to feel. They think they can get along without it. But in the long run, it is our greatest need of all.

A woman was about to undergo exploratory surgery. Naturally she was concerned. If her condition was really serious, she could lose her health, her hard-earned savings, even life itself. She had heard her pastor tell about the boy who misquoted Psalm 23. She knew this was the one security nothing could take from her. So, as she was taken to the operating room, she said to herself over and over again, "The Lord is my shepherd, that's all I want."

"The Lord is my shepherd, that's all I want."

Kept in the Eye of God

In his book *A Window in Thrums,* Sir James Barrie tells about an old Scottish mother who sat in an invalid's chair by her window watching the people as they went back and forth in front of her house. Often a King James Bible lay on her lap, opened to Genesis 16:13. In memory she saw a young son who had announced he was going to be a minister. He had even chosen as the text for his first sermon, "Thou God seest me," Genesis 16:13.

He never got to preach that sermon, for he was killed in a tragic accident. His mother confessed that for a long time she could not read his text. But now it had become her favorite text in the Bible.

The text comes out of Hagar's experience. Thinking she could not bear children to Abraham, Sarah suggested that Abraham take her servant Hagar as a second wife. When Hagar became pregnant with Abraham's child, she became so arrogant toward Sarah that Sarah, with Abraham's permission, ordered Hagar out of the house.

Desolate, Hagar wandered to a nearby oasis to ponder her fate. In her loneliness she felt God's presence telling her to return to Sarah and apologize, and that Sarah would forgive her and welcome her back. Confident that God had not forgotten her, Hagar gratefully lifted her eyes to heaven, and said, "Thou God seest me."

This was a favorite text with Puritan ministers, but they used it to scare people into being good. They made it sound like "Big Brother is watching you." Of course, that isn't what Hagar meant at all. She meant that God had not forsaken her. God knew where she was, and God was there to guide her.

God never loses us in a crowd. Wherever we go, the Psalmist assures us, we are under God's watchcare (Psalm 139:9-10). A woman was asked how she could sleep so well when she had so many problems. She said, "The Bible tells me that God neither slumbers nor sleeps. So I say, 'God, you're going to be awake anyhow. There's no use for both of us to lose sleep over my problems.' So I turn over and go to sleep."

Whose Yoke Are You Wearing?

A boy was playing in a barn when he saw an old-fashioned ox yoke. It was very heavy, but he found he could lift it. So he carried it out into the barnyard where he put one end of it over the head of a calf. Then, to add to the fun, he put his own head through the other end. This was more fun for him than for the calf. The calf let out a bellow and began running across the barnyard, dragging the boy with it. Hanging on to the yoke with all his strength to keep from being strangled, the boy yelled at the top of his voice, "Somebody catch us! We're running away!"

That's the way a lot of us feel these days. We feel yoked to a world that is running away and is dragging us toward greater inflation, permissiveness, and crime, a world that is threatening to strangle many of the time-honored virtues that have made life worth living.

When Jesus offered his yoke to people, he was not offering it to those who were not wearing any. He offered it *in exchange* for the intolerable burdens they were already bearing. He offered forgiveness in exchange for guilt; inner peace in exchange for bitterness and resentment; faith instead of fear, and hope in exchange for despair.

To accept his yoke is to receive forgiveness for our crushing weight of guilt. It is to receive the joy of his presence in place of the loneliness of facing life and death without his help.

Remember the words of Jesus: "Take my yoke upon you and learn of me; for I am gentle and lowly in heart, and you will find rest for your souls" (Matthew 11:29).

Sermons from Bumper Stickers

A Baptist church in Atlanta was having trouble with people, who were not church members, parking in its parking lot. Some young people solved the problem by putting bumper stickers on all the cars. The bumper sticker read, "It's great to be a Baptist."

Religion is sometimes proclaimed by bumper stickers. One such sticker said, "If you love Jesus, honk." Another said, "If you love Jesus, tithe. Anyone can honk."

One bumper sticker that was popular for a while said, "I found it." Its purpose was to serve as a conversation starter. When anyone asked, "What have you found?" the driver or owner of the car could reply, "Peace through knowing Jesus."

Have *you* found it? John Wesley, the founder of Methodism, did. He was an ordained clergyman, but something was missing. One evening, he attended a prayer meeting in a chapel on Aldersgate Street in London, and as he heard the minister read Martin Luther's interpretation of acceptance with God through faith, he felt his heart being "strangely warmed." He went all over England proclaiming his heartwarming message.

William Carey, the first modern missionary to India, found it. As a youth, he made fun of a fellow worker's faith. The boy invited him to his church. He went out of curiosity, and for the first time felt what he later called "experiential religion."

There is a further question that needs to be asked. If you have found it, does your life show it? How is your life different because you found it? Do others see a difference between you and those who don't even bother to look for it?

An Experiment that Works

In her biography of Thomas A. Edison, Mary Childs Nerny says that "a man on the Homeric scale cannot be measured by a slide rule." By whatever measurement you use, Edison was a genius. His genius would have spun off into thin air, however, if it had not been for his hard work and dogged persistence.

Convinced that, if he could find the right substance to use as a filament, he could invent an electric light, Edison set out to find a substance that could combine a small diameter with a high resistance to electric current. Before he discovered that tungsten would work, he had tried almost three thousand metals and fibers.

After seven hundred failures, one of his fellow workers advised him to give up. "We have tried seven hundred things," said the worker, "and haven't found out a thing." "Oh, yes we have," replied Mr. Edison. "We have found out seven hundred things that don't work.

A Bible writer known only as "The Preacher" tells us of the things that did not work in his life (Ecclesiastes 1-5). He tried education, but education alone did not work. Though an educated sinner, he was still a sinner. He tried folly, but that didn't work either. He even tried alcohol, but that certainly didn't work. He tried wealth. He became the richest person Jerusalem had ever known. But even that didn't work. He found he couldn't buy happiness. He complained that a poor man can sleep while a rich man lies awake worrying about his money.

Then he tried God. To his surprise, that worked. So much so, that he pleads with young people to remember their Creator in the days of their youth so that they need not face days that "have no pleasure in them" because they have no hope (Ecclesiastes 12:1).

Push or Pull?

When the Marquis of Wellesley, Governor General of India at the time, and a brother-in-law of the Duke of Wellington, heard that William Carey was translating the Bible into the native dialect, he was greatly disturbed, and said he could not allow it. When asked why, he explained, "The Bible teaches that all men are on a level. It will never do to give these natives the idea that they are equal to us, or it will be farewell to British rule in India."

Voicing his opposition to Mr. Carey, he said, "Do you not think it is wrong to force these natives to become Christians?" Mr. Carey replied, "Sir, the thing is impossible. We can indeed force a person to become a hypocrite. But no power on earth can force a person to become a Christian."

God does not shove; God attracts. God does not say, "Everyone must come," but "whosoever will may come." God did not push Abraham out of Ur. Abraham was pulled by a conviction that God wanted him to launch out. David was not forced to write his Psalms. He wanted to write them because of what God had done for him.

We can never force a person to agree with us; we can only try to win his agreement by persuasion. We cannot force others to become our friends; we must win their friendship. And we cannot force another to become a Christian. We must make the Christian life so attractive that others will want to become Christians, too.

7

The Lure of Temptation

It was *after* the glorious experience of God's approval had come to him at the time of his baptism that Jesus was most grievously tempted. Temptations do not stop when one becomes a Christian. Indeed, they can become more subtle as the Christian is tempted to neglect or compromise his or her witness.

In an amazingly frank disclosure of his own inner life, the apostle Paul gives us a look at his own ongoing battle with temptation. He has already declared his pride in following Christ (Romans 1:16). He has described how faith in Christ enables one to become a new person (Romans 6:6). Now, in a moment of frank confession, he speaks of his continuing battle to do the right. Listen to his words in Romans 7:15-23 (TEV):

> I do not understand what I do; for I don't do what I would like to do, but instead I do what I hate. . . . For even though the desire to do good is in me, I am not able to do it. I don't do the good I want to do; instead, I do the evil that I do not want to do. . . . When I want to do what is good, what is evil is the only choice I have. My inner being delights in the law of God. But I see a different law at work in my body—a law that fights against the law which my mind approves of. It makes me a prisoner to the law of sin which is at work in my body.

Paul indulged in this candor not just to raise the issue, but because he knew the answer. He knew where to turn when temptation comes. He knew who would rescue him from defeat. He knew from whom the help would come. It would come from God through the saving message and power of Jesus Christ (Romans 7:25). That is why Paul could also write, "God keeps his promise, and he will not allow you to be tested beyond your power to remain firm; at the time you are put to the test, he will give you the strength to endure it, and so provide you with a way out" (1 Corinthians 10:13, TEV).

Nevertheless, temptation is real. Everyone, Christians included, needs to be on constant guard against its lure. Not just temptations of the baser sort, but the more subtle temptations to compromise one's convictions and ideals; the nagging temptations to seek human approval rather than God's.

In this battle one needs the whole arsenal of God's weapons. One needs the help of the Holy Spirit. One needs a knowledge of the Bible. One needs the power of prayer. One also needs the encouragement and support of other Christians in the church, people who like oneself are waging the battle to do right and who look to God and the church to help them win the victory.

The following illustrations turn the spotlight of attention on this important phase of Christian living.

Beware the Leopard

It sounds absolutely incredible, but a not-very-recent issue of the Holiday Inn magazine *Companion* tells about a car thief who vows he will never steal another car because of what happened the last time he tried to steal one.

Seeing a new car, he managed to break into it and start the motor. What he didn't know was that the car belonged to a wild-animal trainer. He was so intent on what he was doing that he failed to notice a pet leopard asleep on the back seat. As he started off, the motion of the car wakened the leopard, and it jumped over into the front seat beside him. One can imagine his panic when he saw the leopard, and the mad scramble with which he must have tried to get out of that car and shut the door.

Temptation to sin always tries to focus our attention on the shining attraction of some sinful desire. It fails to mention the danger sleeping in the background. But the danger is there. Call it guilt, or call it fear of being found out, but when it is aroused it can destroy our happiness and peace of mind.

Satan tried to dazzle Jesus by holding up the glittering prospect of misusing his power to satisfy mere appetite (his own and others'), and of using Satan's methods of trying to subjugate the world rather than God's way of trying to save the world. But Jesus saw the danger lurking behind every enticement, and refused to put his soul in jeopardy.

At Calvary the bestial forces of hate, vilification, and torture were all turned against Jesus, but they could not make him turn aside from God's purpose for his life. They could not make him hate back. If threats could not defeat him, surely death could. But even death failed to conquer him. Jesus—not sin, not death, but Jesus—came off the victor.

He has promised to share that victory with us. The guilt we cannot shrug off, he promises to forgive. The happiness we cannot steal, he offers as a gift.

The Devil Wears a False Face

A child dressed up like an angel, and went begging on trick-or-treat night. At one house, he got a big cookie. At the next house, a woman dropped an apple in his sack. When he saw that the apple had broken the cookie, he forgot the meaning of his costume and cursed at her.

He didn't know it, but he was acting like Satan. For, as the Bible tells us, Satan himself likes to masquerade as an angel of light (2 Corinthians 11:14). He hides his evil nature behind a benign appearance. He presents temptation in an attractive form so as to disguise its latent dangers.

For example, he likes to wear his "just this once" grin. "I'm not asking you to get hooked on drugs," he smirks. "Just smoke this one marijuana cigarette to see how it excites your mind."

Or there is his "everybody's doing it" false face. Or his "you can get away with it" disguise. "Other people get caught," he says from behind what he hopes will be a disarming smile, "but you're different—you're smart." Or "Your body is different. You'll be one of the lucky ones who can get away with it."

How different it is when we turn to Jesus! Everything about him was on the level. There was not a deceitful cell in his body. He didn't *pretend* to love us. He *loved* us, and proved it by going to the cross for us. He didn't *pretend* to suffer and die, he *suffered and died*—and rose again from the dead.

In fact, the thing he hated most of all was hypocrisy. No mask of pretense, no make-believe piety is ever acceptable to him. He wants utter sincerity in our response to his love.

Satan promises freedom and delivers slavery. Jesus asks for obedience and delivers freedom.

Watch Out for Spiders

A certain man had a favorite prayer he liked to repeat in prayer meeting. He would pray, "Dear God, brush away the cobwebs from my life that I may see thee more clearly." Once, after he had said this for the umpteenth time, a woman rose and prayed, "Yes, Lord, do grant our brother's request, and this time please kill the spider."

Spiders amaze me. When my wife and I clean our house, we have a special attachment for the vacuum sweeper that gets into the corners. But often, a few days after we think it has been cleaned thoroughly, we look, and lo, a new cobweb has appeared in the corner.

Where do spiders come from? What do they eat? It almost seems as if they know to run and hide when they hear a vacuum sweeper. Even if we ask God to kill the spider, more little spiders seem to show up.

In a way, life is like that. We ask forgiveness so that we may present a clean life to God. Then, to our dismay, out pops an ugly thought, an ugly attitude, and we need to pray again for God's forgiveness and help. That is why, even when we have committed our life to God, we need God's daily presence, daily forgiveness, and daily love to help us deal with our daily temptations.

No Laughter in Hell

A man once told a funny story about hell in the presence of Dwight L. Moody. When the laughter had subsided, Mr. Moody quietly remarked, "If you must speak about hell, do it with tears in your eyes."

Jerry Clower would agree. Jerry Clower entertains audiences with his rural Mississippi brand of humor. Once after people had laughed uproariously at some of his humor, he became serious and said, "There's one place where there isn't any laughter, and that's hell."

No laughter in hell! I have often said that one reason I want to go to heaven is that there are no children in the other place. And here is a humorist reminding us that there is no laughter there, either. No children! No laughter! No joy of being in God's presence! Who wants to spend eternity in such a repulsive place?

Yet millions go blithely on, ignoring all the warnings of Scripture. Evidently they think God is too softhearted to punish them. But it was Jesus himself who spoke of a "furnace of fire" where "men will weep and gnash their teeth" (Matthew 13:42).

The Bible is clear about it. "Do not be deceived; God is not mocked: for whatever a man sows, that he will also reap" (Galatians 6:7). "The wages of sin is death" (Romans 6:23). "For what will it profit a man, if he gains the whole world and forfeits his life?" (Matthew 16:26). These are ominous words. As Jerry Clower would say, "They are no laughing matter."

No laughter! no joy! no peace of mind! no hope! Who wants to spend five minutes, let alone eternity, in such an awful place? God doesn't want us to spend eternity there. That's why God sent Jesus to show us a better way in this world and the way to a heavenly life in the hereafter.

How Do You Punctuate Your Life?

In a Washington suburb there is a famous restaurant called Mrs. K's Toll House Tavern. Over the fireplace there is this sentence: "If the B empty put: If the B . putting :" Decoded, it reads, "If the B (great B) empty put : (colon). If the B (great B) . (the period means full stop) putting : (colon)." In other words, "If the grate be empty, put coal on. If the grate be full, stop putting coal on."

Taken seriously, punctuation is a very important matter. How a sentence is punctuated can make a big difference in its meaning.

The work of Bible translators is made more difficult by the fact that there was no punctuation in the original languages. For example, did Isaiah mean to put a comma between Wonderful and Counsellor in Isaiah 9:6, as in the King James Version, or did he mean to say "Wonderful Counselor," as in the Revised Standard? Or in Ephesians 4:12, did Paul mean to separate "the perfecting of the saints" with a comma from "the work of the ministry" (as in the King James Version), emphasizing that they are two separate gifts? Or did he mean to say, For the perfecting of the saints for the work of the ministry"? In other words, does God perfect us in saintliness so that we will do the work of ministry? The Revised Standard translators, deciding against the comma, rendered the passage as "to equip the saints for the work of ministry."

As we look at evidences of God's handiwork, we often feel like reaching for exclamation points. How amazing! How wonderful! When we see so much suffering and evil in the world, we feel like reaching for a question mark. Why? But sometimes we need a comma to remind us of the need for a pause in our lives, "Be still, and know that I am God" (Psalm 46:10). And if there is a known sin in our lives, we need a period to remind us to bring it to a full stop. "If thy right eye causes you to sin, pluck it out and throw it away" (Matthew 5:29). Better a complete stop to sin than to make a dash after an evil that can separate us from God.

8
Repentance and Forgiveness

President Warren G. Harding attended the Calvary Baptist Church when he was in the White House, but he would never attend on Communion Sunday. He once explained to Dr. William S. Abernethy, the pastor at that time, that he stayed away because he did not feel worthy to partake of the Lord's Supper.

The fact is that no one goes to church because he or she is worthy. We all go to church, or should go to church, to confess our unworthiness and to pray for another chance to do better.

Without the assurance of God's forgiveness, we'd all end up under the curse of guilt. Psychiatrists' couches would be full of unhelped and unhealed patients, because there is no substitute for forgiveness of a guilty conscience.

Without forgiveness Christ's perfection would be an offense, for it would only serve to remind us of our miserable imperfections. Without forgiveness God's moral law would drive us to desperation because it demands of us a perfection we are not capable of achieving. Without forgiveness Christ's example would be our despair, because we can never fully attain to it.

But Christ's love is a cleansing love. He did not wait until we were worthy and lovable before he loved us, or he would have had to wait forever. The astounding good news of the gospel is that "while we were yet sinners" Christ loved us enough to die for us (Romans 5:8). That declaration, which is not just a challenge to try harder, but something infinitely greater, is what constitutes good news for a sinner.

Repentance on our part and forgiveness on God's part are absolutely indispensable to Christian living. Following are some illustrations that highlight this very important truth.

A Faith that Rescues

A young girl attended a young people's assembly where I was the vesper speaker. On the first night I tried to hold up Jesus as our perfect example. As I talked, the girl began to feel miserable. She had soiled her life, and the more I talked about the purity and perfection of Jesus, the worse she felt. I spoke no word of condemnation. I spoke only of the beauty of Jesus. But in the light of his purity she condemned herself. After the service, she told me later, she went to her room and wept bitter tears.

She almost stayed away from the service the second night, but at the last minute, she told me, she decided to come. That evening I told a legend about a man who walked too close to the edge of a precipice and fell over. He managed to catch hold of a protruding root. He had fallen too far to climb back by his own efforts, and if he let go, he would fall to his death. His only hope was for someone to rescue him, so he began to call for help.

Gautama Buddha heard his call and looked over the precipice. He gave him some good advice for living, but walked on and left him hanging there. Confucius did the same. The man called out again, his strength almost gone. This time Jesus looked over the precipice. Seeing the man's plight, he got down on the ground, and reaching down got hold of the man and pulled him back to safety.

For the second time in a row, the girl told me, she went to her room and cried. But this time they were tears of penitence and joy. Now she saw Jesus not only as an unattainable ideal, but as a loving Savior. As she asked him to lift her up, she felt clean again.

Speaking to the students at the Northern Baptist Seminary in Chicago, Dr. David Augsburger once said, "Nothing arouses a concrete and responsible awareness of guilt like an exposure to grace. My experience is that I feel free to confess when I feel cared for and know that forgiveness is potential."

The Universal Plague

In her book *Bathsheba,* Roberta Kells Dor imagines a conversation between Nathan the prophet and David the king. Nathan has accused David of murder and wife-stealing. Conscience-stricken, David has sought God's forgiveness. Nathan points out that there were others also implicated in David's sin. In reply David comments, "It seems there aren't just two kinds of men, those who sin and those who do not. There are only those who seek forgiveness, and those who do not."

How right he was! And yet one of the problems faced by every evangelist or pastor in trying to lead persons to Christ, the Great Physician, is first to convince them that they are sick. Jesus faced the same problem in dealing with religious people in his day. The Pharisees knew the publicans and sinners were sick, but they failed to realize that *they themselves* were infected with the virus of self-righteousness. To Jesus it was very evident. It was evident in their feverish pride, in the way their blood pressure rose when he spoke favorably of Syrians and Sidonites, in the chill they experienced when he healed people on the Sabbath.

The Pharisees needed to recognize the universality of sin. No one is immune from its virus. That is why we need the healing power of God's forgiveness, a transfusion of God's love, the therapy of prayer, and an exercise of compassion toward others.

Someone has said, "God loves you just as you are, but God loves you too much to leave you that way." This statement applies to every living person. There is no one who does not need a daily appointment with Jesus. His grace can heal and keep us well.

Sharing in Death
and Resurrection

$\mathbf{A}$ young girl had indulged in many sins. Through the witness of a friend and the grace of God, she was truly converted. However, her old crowd didn't understand what had happened to her. They thought she wasn't having any fun anymore, so they invited her to one of their parties.

Knowing that many of her former friends were on drugs and alcohol, she sought the advice of a Christian friend. She said, "I don't enjoy those things anymore. What excuse should I give them for not going to their party?"

The Christian friend said, "Thank them for inviting you, but tell them you can't come because you're dead."

"Dead?" said the surprised girl. Then her face lighted up, and she said, "That's right. The person they knew is dead. I'm a different person now. In fact, my church was so sure I died, it actually buried me in the watery grave of baptism, and I rose to live a new kind of life with Christ."

Not all churches practice baptism by immersion, but this was undoubtedly the kind of baptism Paul had in mind when he wrote Romans 6:3-4. Paul used this illustration as a warning against superficial repentance. True repentance, he pointed out, means a willingness to die—to be buried—to a life of sin and indifference, and a desire to be resurrected to a new life with Christ.

To those who asked, "Why, then, can we not go on sinning, knowing that God will forgive us when we ask?" Paul had two answers. First, a truly penitent person would never think that way. He would no longer enjoy sinning. His joy would now be found in serving the Lord. Second, "The wages of sin is death" (Romans 6:23). Sin is an infection. One does not fool around with an infection. Unless it is cured, it can lead to death.

Destructive Children

I wouldn't mind those children coming here if they weren't so destructive." The speaker was a church trustee who, as a member of the board, shared the responsibility of keeping the physical property in good shape. He was talking about the programs that attracted children of downtown Washington off the streets.

I sympathized with his feelings. After all, church furniture costs money and should be treated with respect. "But," I reminded him, "most of these children come from homes where there is very little furniture, and they are not taught to respect what little furniture they have. If we have to wait until they are perfect little ladies and gentlemen before we let them come, they already are lost. Their only hope is for someone to love them as they are for the sake of what they can become with the right kind of guidance and love."

That, of course, is our hope, too. If God had to wait until we were perfect before loving us, we'd never know God's love. But the Bible assures us of God's love toward us, in that *while we were yet sinners,* Christ died for us (Romans 5:8).

But someone may object, "I try to live a decent, respectable life. Why should I think of myself as a sinner?" Dr. Frank Gaebelein illustrates it this way: When Edmund Hillary stood on the top of Mt. Everest, he was the highest person in the world, but he was still hundreds of thousands of miles away from the nearest star. No matter how good we try to be, we are still light-years away from the perfection of God, and from the perfect obedience of Christ.

In fact, if we flatter ourselves by thinking we are not sinners, we are guilty of the greatest sin of all—pride. This, more than any other thing, keeps us from reaching out in love to our neighbor. It is Christ's forgiving love that sets us free to love both God and our neighbor.

An Organ, a Bell, and a Clock

Much of the money for the historic sanctuary of the Calvary Baptist Church in Washington, D. C., was given by Amos Kendall, who served as postmaster general under Presidents Andrew Jackson and Martin Van Buren. When he retired from public life, he became the lawyer for Samuel F. B. Morse, the inventor of the telegraph.

In giving the money, Mr. Kendall stipulated that when the church building was built, it must have in it "an organ, a bell, and a clock."

I have always been glad that he asked for those three things in that order. First, the organ reminds us of the need for harmony in our world. There is need of harmony between nations, between races, between capital and labor, between the old and young, and even between religious groups. There is need for harmony between the conflicting passions within ourselves.

But an organ can produce harmony only if a gifted organist is at the keyboard. That is why we need the bell to call us back to God. Only God can produce the harmony we need as God turns the dissonance of self-will into the harmony of love for God and neighbor. Only God, by forgiveness, can turn the clashing discords of sin and guilt into the harmony of inner peace.

The clock reminds us that we do not have forever in this world to serve God. When a moment passes, it is gone forever; it brings us that much closer to the time when we must give an accounting of whether we have preferred the dissonances of sin and self-will or the harmony of commitment to God and God's will.

From Cellar to Attic

William Barclay tells about a woman in Edinburgh who lived in a cellar room amidst filthy conditions. The Rev. George Matheson came to be the minister of her church. Sometime later, an elder from the church went to visit her and found she had moved. He later located her in an attic room. Her furnishings were still meager, but the room was sunny, airy, and clean. "I see you have changed your house," said the elder. "Aye," the woman replied, "You canna hear George Matheson preach and live in a cellar."

Obviously, George Matheson preached with winsomeness and power, but it was his message that was supremely important. It was Christ who made the woman dissatisfied with her cellar surroundings. We are quick to say that Jesus satisfies, but he first makes us dissatisfied with ourselves and the world as we are. As someone has put it, he must first make us unhappy sinners before he can make us happy saints.

He changes us by making us *want* a new life. Where we once enjoyed, or endured, uncleanness in and around us, we now want to live on a higher and cleaner level. Where we once looked with indifference on sinfulness and indulgence, we now want a life consistent with him who is altogether lovely. Where we were once content with the cellar of injustice, we now want the sunshine of justice to shine on our world. Where we have lived in a cellar of despair, we now feel the fresh air of hope blowing across our lives.

The Art of Beginning Again

In his book *Beginnings Without End* Sam Keen tells about a dream he once had after certain events had changed his life. In this dream a man appeared to him and said, "I have learned one important thing in my life—how to begin again."

We all have times when we face the need of a new beginning. We sin and need to repent. We fall and need to try again. A marriage comes apart, and two people must make separate lives for themselves. A loved one dies, and those left must learn to live with the void. A person loses a job and is faced with the traumatic experience of finding and beginning a new one. A person or family moves and must adjust to new surroundings. A person loses his health or grows old, and must adjust to a new lifestyle.

Fear of rejection often adds to the mental anguish of those who have made a mistake. This is where the church needs to be supportive.

One thing is certain. The Bible assures us that when we seek another chance God is always willing to give it to us. As God came to Jonah a second time (Jonah 3:1-2), so God will come to us a second, a third, a fourth, and so on, seeking to draw us into divine love and will.

There is, however, a warning. Some people think that, even if they disregard God to the very end of their lives, God will still give them another chance after death; that because God is love and has all eternity at God's disposal, God will not give up till the last sinner has responded to divine love.

This is an appealing idea to those who do not want to change their ways, but it is a dangerous gamble to take. If there is such a promise in the Bible, it is hard to find. On the contrary, the Bible talks about a gulf in eternity so wide and deep that, in spite of his remorse, a man who had been callous and indifferent on earth could not cross over (Luke 16:20-26). Why take a chance?

Memories that Bless and Burn

An absent-minded person looked at his engagement calendar and said, "Oh, no! I had a dinner engagement last week, and I forgot all about it." So he called the hostess and apologized profusely for forgetting. "But," said the hostess in a puzzled tone, "you were here."

Memory is a priceless gift. Without it the past would be as unknown as the future. Nothing more tragic can happen to anyone than for that person to lose his or her memory. Memory enables us to relive our golden hours. It can give us guidance from the past to help us live more wisely in the present. Memory enables us to recall those who have gone before us. No wonder Sir James Barrie said, "God gave us memory so that we might have roses in December."

Memories can burn as well as bless. A young man who had lived a sinful life said in despair, "I wish to God I could forget some things." Of course, he couldn't forget. Not even Christ could make him forget his sinful past, but Christ can do something infinitely more important. When we ask him, he can forgive our past sins, thereby taking the sting out of our memories. He can enable us to begin a new life with him.

The time to build beautiful memories is now. It is today's experiences that become tomorrow's memories. Some years ago, a young music lover pawned his overcoat to buy a ticket to hear Paderewski play a piano recital. He had to wear extra shirts under his suit to keep warm, but, he never regretted his action. "Every time I remember that concert," he says, "I draw another dividend from the bank of my memory."

Good intentions do not build beautiful memories, nor are we remembered for our good intentions. We are remembered for what we do. The disciples did not remember Jesus' resurrection because of his words. It was the other way around: They remembered his words because of his resurrection (John 12:16). People remember what we do long after they have forgotten what we say.

Rain in the Face

Whether this actually happened or not, it makes a good story. When Dr. Merton Rice was pastor of the Metropolitan Methodist Church in Detroit, Michigan, he is said to have asked his friend Bishop Quayle how he managed to keep his spiritual vitality at such a high peak all the time.

The bishop replied that he did what all good Christians are supposed to do. He read his Bible, said his prayers, and went to church. "And," he said, "some things speak to me especially of God. For example, I like to walk in the rain. I like to throw back my head, and let the rain fall on my face, and I get a revelation."

Sometime later, the two men met again. Dr. Rice said to his friend, "You and your ideas!" He said, "It rained the other day, and, remembering what you said, I went out and walked in the rain. I threw back my head, and let the rain fall on my face. The water ran down my neck. I didn't get any revelation. I felt like a fool." "Well," said the Bishop, "what more of a revelation do you want the first time than that?"

We've all had revelations of this sort, and it didn't take rain in the face to do it. Who, at times, has not been reminded of his fallibility?

Sometimes this kind of insight is good for us. It punctures our pride. At times we need to have humbling experiences. Of course, they can go too far. We can experience self-depreciation to the point of giving up.

Therefore, along with revelations of our unworthiness, we also need revelations of our worth. This is where Jesus gives us the proper balance. He humbles us. Who can feel proud when he compares himself to Jesus? But Jesus also gives us the highest revelation of our worth. He showed us by his death that he thought we were worth dying for.

A Bird in the Study

I walked into my study, and to my very great surprise a white-throated sparrow flew across the room. How it got in I do not know. It must have flown in through the door when we were bringing groceries in from the car. We closed the doors and opened a window, and soon the frightened bird flew to freedom.

What terror must have been in the little bird's breast when it found itself trapped in a room with a huge creature called man. If it only knew that the last thing I wanted to do was to hurt it. In fact, it was I who opened the window and made it possible for the bird to fly to freedom.

Many a sinner feels trapped by his sin. Down deep he wants to escape, but doesn't know how. He even is afraid to turn to God. *Surely God would want to take away his pleasure and punish him for his sins,* he thinks. If he only knew that God doesn't want to hurt him, but to save him. God wants to keep him from hurting himself by flying against the hard walls of whatever may be his temptation. God wants to guide him toward the open window of God's love, so he can find his way to a new freedom.

How wonderful the sun and the air must have felt to the freed little bird. Once again it could fly as God meant it to fly. Once again it was close to the sheltering protection of trees. The person who finds his way back to God finds a similar freedom. Fear has given way to faith. Once again his spirit can soar. Once again he can settle on the branches of self-respect and experience the joy of feeling the wind of God's Spirit around him.

We get trapped by so many things—our fears, our doubts, our prejudices, our sins. We need to find the open window of God's love, so we can soar to new heights of spiritual growth and inspire others with our song of joy.

For Whom Does the Rooster Crow?

There is an amusing story of a man who got on an elevator to go down from his apartment. On the next floor a man got on the elevator holding a crate of chickens. "What are you doing with those chickens?" asked the first man. "I've had them in my apartment," the other replied, "but the management tells me I must get rid of them." The first man fainted. When he came to, the other man asked him, "Are you allergic to chickens?" "No," replied the first man, "but yesterday I paid a psychiatrist $300 to convince my wife that she was not hearing a rooster crowing."

In Jerusalem, even today, one can often hear a rooster crowing. This sound comes as a surprise to American tourists who live in cities where raising chickens is forbidden. The early morning crowing of a rooster reminds one of another rooster in Jerusalem a long time ago. Its crowing not only announced the coming of the dawn but reminded a disciple of Jesus that his master had predicted he would break under pressure.

In Jerusalem today the Church of St. Peter in Gallincantu commemorates Peter's denial. A large metal silhouette of a rooster is perched on top of the cross that is mounted on the dome-shaped tower of the church. Perhaps we need such a symbol on top of some of our churches today. Not just a cross, but a cross and a rooster to remind us of the times when we, too, have denied the Master and have been unfaithful to his cause. Such a sight might enable us to hear a crowing-like sound deep in our own conscience. Then we too could turn to Christ in deeper penitence and dedication to his cause.

9

The Power of Prayer

A missionary who had spent several years in Japan returned to the United States. I asked her what impressed her most about the churches in the States. Her response was immediate. "The lack of agonizing prayer," she said.

She went on to point out that in Japan, where Christians are so greatly outnumbered, where their resources are so limited, and where the bulk of the people are indifferent, if not actually hostile, to the Christian message, Christians know they cannot impress the people with the size and wealth of their churches. They have to depend on God for their victories. So they fairly besiege God with their prayers. And often, she said, they feel their prayers are answered in almost miraculous ways.

Most churches in the United States need more prayer power—more times when people gather together to pray—more people who pray believing that God hears and answers prayer. As the missionary said, they need more "agonizing prayer," more confessing, more joyous thanksgiving, more earnest seeking for the will of God, more willingness to be filled with, and guided by, the Holy Spirit.

The more successful a church is in terms of this world's standards, the more members it has, the more impressive buildings it can build, the more it is often tempted to neglect its prayer life. Activities are important and essential, but they must not be allowed to crowd out prayer time. Blessed is the church that has a praying pastor who encourages his or her people to pray.

Dr. George Buttrick was for many years the gifted minister of the Madison Avenue Presbyterian church in New York City. He was known far and wide as an outstanding preacher. But he once told me that it was his regular practice to go into his empty sanctuary on Saturday evening, and, knowing many of the people who would be sitting there the following day, he would move from pew to pew and pray for the people to whom he would be preaching on the following morning. In that way he expressed to God his love and concern for his people and kept his own heart sensitive to their needs.

In this book we speak of the centrality of Christ, the need for inner renewal, the ministry of the Holy Spirit, the lure of temptation, the need to reach out to others, and many elements of the faith. But how can we emulate Christ if we do not pray? How can we experience inner renewal if we do not pray? How can we be sensitive to the leading of God's Spirit if we do not pray? How can we be strengthened in the face of temptation if we do not pray? How can we do all we can for others if we do not pray for them?

In writing to the Philippians Paul wrote, "I am sure that he who began a good work in you will bring it to completion at the day of Jesus Christ" (Philippians 1:6). Prayer is one of the most valuable aids, if not the most valuable, to Christian growth. The following illustrations call attention to the supreme importance of prayer in the life of a Christian.

The Wind and the Sail

A sailor was telling a small boy about the sea. He mentioned the wind. "What's wind?" asked the little boy. "I don't know what wind is," replied the sailor, "but I know what it does when I raise a sail."

We now know a lot about how to chart the wind's course, but we still can't see it; we can only see what it does. So it is with God's Spirit. We can't see it; we can only see what it does in the lives of those who put their trust in God.

The winds of God's grace are always blowing, but we must raise the sail of faith if we want them to propel us toward deeper peace and joy.

Prayer is lifting our sails to the winds of God's wisdom and power. We do not tell the wind which way to blow. We learn how to adjust our sail to the wind so it can propel us in the right direction. In prayer we do not tell God how to act. Instead, we lift our praise and concerns so God can fill us with a deeper sense of God's presence and help us steer toward the answer God has in store for us.

Let Us Pray

When Clarence Jordan, the founder of the Koinonia Farm in Americus, Georgia, was a student in seminary, he first went to the library to get books. He soon found himself going for more books than he could read because they gave him an excuse to talk to the librarian. In time, he often went to the library not to get books at all but to see the librarian. Later on, he married her.

Many people pray only when they want something from God. The more they become committed to God, however, the more they find themselves turning to prayer, not to ask for something, but to commune with God.

Prayer means many things. For one thing, it is a way of working with God. In his book *Intercessory Prayer,* Dr. Edward Bauman says that God is at work in every situation, but prayer changes the situation. It actually gives God a new situation with which to work.

Dr. Frank Laubach used to say that the Holy Spirit is trying to break through into every situation, but often is kept from doing so because there is no conducive atmosphere of sincere, persistent prayer.

Moreover, prayer is a way of showing God we care. In Isaiah 59:16 there is the statement that God wondered that there was no one to intervene. God must wonder at our silence. God must feel like saying, "You say you care. You say you have faith. Then why don't you show it by praying for those persons and situations about which you are concerned?"

Above all, prayer is a way of cultivating a deeper awareness of the presence of God. We may not always get the answer we want, but prayer can help us to accept God's answer, knowing that we have God's love.

Growing in Prayer

Some years ago, after a critical time in his own life when he discovered the importance of prayer, Harry Emerson Fosdick wrote a book entitled *The Meaning of Prayer*. Among other things, he reminded us that the prayer of the prodigal son changed from "give me" to "make me."

First the young man prayed, "Give me the share of property that falls to me" (Luke 15:12). When he received what he asked for, he spent it all for selfish pleasure and landed in a pigsty. When he came to his senses, though, his prayer became "treat me as one of your hired servants" (Luke 15:19). He was willing to be made a slave if that was his father's will, but that was not necessary. Because of his father's love, he was welcomed back as a member of the family.

So often we think of prayer as a means of trying to get what we want instead of a means of letting God direct our lives. Therefore, Dr. Fosdick reminded us that in Gethsemane, Jesus did not pray to change God's will. Instead, his prayer was "not my will, but thine, be done" (Luke 22:42).

We often pray as if we were trying to change God's mind. Of course, we can express our desires to God. Jesus did. True prayer, however, does not try to change God's will. Rather, it seeks to discover God's will and to be led to the desire to obey it.

Where have we arrived in prayer? At "give me" or "make me"? At "thy will be changed" or "thy will be done"? It is not always easy to make the transition from the one to the other, yet the effectiveness of our prayer life depends on our willingness to seek and accept God's will.

Let's Get This Over

Dr. C. Oscar Johnson used to say that his church was not bothered by postmillennialists and premillennialists. What bothered him most was the "postdoxologists" and the "prebenedictionists." He was referring to the people who rush into church after the service has started, and rush out after the last verse of the last hymn without waiting for the benediction.

There are times when any person gets held up on his way to church or has to leave early to keep an appointment. Dr. Johnson, however, was talking about people who are always in a hurry, rushing in at the last minute, rushing out at the first opportunity, begrudging the time they set aside for the worship of God.

Hurry, hurry, hurry! Too busy for God. Too busy to spend much time in God's presence. That's the way most of us live these days. Our forefathers walked on the good earth. They heard the birds sing, watched the foliage grow, felt the presence of God everywhere. We speed to work over hard asphalt, our hands gripping the steering wheel, our eyes glued on the rear bumper of the car ahead. How can we have time for God when so much of our time is taken up with getting through the day?

Even worse, many people do not have time for one another anymore. Parents work and children get caught up in all their activities. Who has time to sit and talk things out? Even when they do sit, they succumb to the tyranny of television. Who can talk or listen to a loved one while he or she is watching a program on television?

"Be still!" said the psalmist. Stillness takes planning. Unless one is retired or living alone, one has to plan to fit a quiet time into a busy schedule.

Be still, and what? "Be still, and know that I am God" (Psalm 46:10). God wants to talk to us. God wants to ask us about our inner life. God wants to ask us about our attitude toward our neighbor, and what we are doing with and for our neighbor. God wants to ask us, as Christ did Peter, if we really love God.

The Dead Sea Does Have an Outlet

Children in Sunday church school often are told that the Dead Sea has no outlet. Therefore, all the salts and minerals that flow into it from the hills to the north are trapped. The sea is so full of these salts and minerals that you could float in the water with only about two-thirds of your body submerged. The rocks along the shore are glazed with salt. In some places salt crystallizes in cakes along the shore. These cakes sometimes break off and float on the water, looking for all the world like cakes of ice floating in the intense heat that is usually found in that area.

Yet Dr. George Buttrick insists that the Dead Sea does have an outlet. Otherwise, where would all the water be that has flowed into this sea for thousands of years? By now it would have inundated most of Palestine, but it hasn't. The surface of the sea remains at a constant level because the water evaporates. In other words, the outlet is upward. The water evaporates, rising in the form of vapor and leaving the sediment behind.

In the same way, says Dr. Buttrick, when we get to the place where we think there is no way out, there is still a way up. We can still turn to God in prayer.

A pastor preached on Psalm 91. At the close of the service, instead of a benediction, he quietly recited the psalm. The next morning he received a phone call from one of his members. She confessed that she had been so worried about personal problems that she had not listened to his sermon. But, as he was reciting the psalm, she said she felt herself relax. She said, "I have hardly slept for a week, but I came home and slept like a baby. I still don't know the way out of my problems, but I have a new confidence that God is going to help me as I look up to God."

Have you read that psalm lately?

Golf at Midnight

Bob Hope tells about a blind golfer. Evidently someone told him the direction in which to hit the ball, and about how far he would have to hit it. He challenged a seeing golfer to play with him. Thinking it would not be much of a challenge, the seeing golfer accepted. "When do you want to start?" asked the man who could see. "At midnight," replied the blind golfer.

It is hard for a seeing person to realize the total darkness in which a blind person constantly lives. The amazing thing is that so many blind people cope so well with their handicap. What they can do, they can do as well in the dark as in the daytime. Even in their darkness, there is the light of learned habit patterns, of cherished friendships, and, if they are believers, of the sense of the presence of God.

Midnight! morning! noon! The time makes no difference to God. After all, God began with the universe when "darkness was upon the face of the deep." God said, "Let there be light," and there was light. Prayer is not limited to daylight hours. God hears those people who cry from the darkness.

The Bible constantly reminds us. Darkness and light are both alike to God (Psalm 139:12). While we sleep, God continues to watch over us (Psalm 121:3-4).

When Paul and Silas were imprisoned in Philippi, they didn't wait till morning to pray and sing. They prayed and sang praises to God *at midnight,* and God heard them (Acts 16:25). So, we are told, did the other prisoners, and they were amazed.

Golf at midnight! Not many of us can do that. But God at midnight! Of course. God is there whenever we need help, for darkness and light are both alike to God.

The Harvest of the Quiet Eye

Borrowing a delightful phrase from Wordsworth, Odell Shepard entitled one of his books *The Harvest of the Quiet Eye.* It is about a two-week walking tour he took through the state of Connecticut. Though he covered twenty to thirty miles a day, he did not hurry. If he met someone who was willing to talk, he stopped to visit with that person. If he felt like sitting under a tree, he sat. If he felt like stretching out on the grass to enjoy the warm sun, he did so. He planned only to reach some inn where he could spend the night.

As he walked or rested, he mused on what he saw and heard. He wrote down his thoughts in a notebook. Thoroughly familiar with the writings of the poets and philosophers of the ages, he laced his musings with quotations from these great thinkers. The jottings stored in his notebook became his book, in which he shows the values of careful observation and quiet reflection on what one sees and hears.

Time! What a priceless gift it is, and how most of us misuse it! The Quakers have felt the importance of listening in silence to the inner voice. Most of us, though, especially in urban society, have not been trained in how to use silence. Indeed, we are lucky if we can find some of it for quiet meditation.

Of course, we can commune with God anywhere. Allen Knights Chalmers, whose days were filled with prayer, tells us that he learned to pray even on a noisy subway train. But some harvests are kept only for those who view them with a quiet eye; who take time to observe, to read, to think, and to pray.

Touch and Go

I didn't see the movie, but I was intrigued by the title: "If This Is Tuesday, It Must Be Belgium."

That is the way many people travel. They go from country to country so fast that they almost have to consult their itinerary to find out what country they are in. It reminds me of the man who boasted that he had gone through the Louvre in three hours, and if he had worn rubber-soled shoes, he could have done it in less time than that.

Imagine giving a Rembrandt painting only a passing glance. Yet some people seem to live like that. When do they slow down long enough to enjoy a flower, to notice a child, to contemplate the meaning of life?

Hymn writer W.D. Longstaff gave us the clue: "Take time to be holy." That's what it takes—time—time to notice, time to appreciate, time to meditate. Time to read the Bible, time to meditate on its meaning, time to pray, time to say thank-you, time to express friendship and love.

To have a happy marriage, one must take time to consider the needs of one's beloved. To have a happy family, parents must take time for the children, time for family discussions, time for family outings.

Many of us live at such a rapid pace that it is hard for us to slow down. We need to take time for God and things of the spirit. How else can we expect to enjoy heaven?

Let the Bus Carry It

A woman got on a bus carrying what seemed to be a rather heavy suitcase. The bus was so crowded that she had to stand near the front. Holding onto a pole with one hand, she continued to hold the suitcase in her other hand. After a while, the bus driver turned to her and said, "Lady, why don't you put down your suitcase and let the bus carry it?"

That was good advice, but the psalmist gives us better advice when he says, "Cast your burden on the Lord, and he will sustain you" (Psalm 55:22).

How do we do that? One way is to think of God's nearness even before we begin to tackle our problems. So often we give God little thought until some problem gets too big for us to handle, and then we call on God to come in and solve it for us. How much better it is to begin with the consciousness of God's willingness to help us find the right answer and to sustain us while we seek for it.

Another way, of course, is to talk things over with God. It often helps us to talk over our problems with another. There are some problems, however, that we may not want to talk over with another human being—not even our most trusted friend. But we can always talk them over with God. In doing so we often experience a peace and guidance that helps us find the answer to which God is leading us.

10

The Value of the Bible

When Dr. George Docherty came to this country from Scotland to fill the pulpit of the New York Avenue Presbyterian Church, the church's old building had been torn down, and a new one was being erected on the same site. During the construction, the congregation worshiped in the Lisner Auditorium of George Washington University. Instead of a regular pulpit, there was a small stand behind which Dr. Docherty stood to preach, and on which the pulpit Bible was placed.

One Sunday, the choir presented a cantata. When Dr. Docherty had finished a brief expository message, a young man came to remove the stand on which the Bible still rested. "Where are you going with the Book?" asked Dr. Docherty. The young man explained that the music director wanted the stand removed. "Put it back," ordered Dr. Docherty. "This is not a religious concert. It is a service of worship, and I want the Bible in the center to remind the people that it is the authority for our Christian message." As he told me of this incident, Dr. Docherty said triumphantly, "The Book stayed in the middle."

The world needs to put the Bible in the center of its thinking and living today. The world needs to give serious attention to the Ten Commandments, the teachings of the prophets, and the Sermon on the Mount and to heed the voice of him who gave that sermon.

The Bible will never be out of date. Styles change. Devices change. The findings of science can soon become outmoded. But the great moral and spiritual teachings of the Bible are as relevant today as when they were first written. The Bible does not care how fast we can travel. It wants to know where we're going. It is not concerned with how much we know about science, as important as that may be. It wants to know what we know about God, and what difference God makes in how we live with each other and with ourselves.

The Book that Speaks to Our Need

A high school student once said to me, "I'd read the Bible more if it were as interesting as the *Reader's Digest.*"

She had not lived very long—or very deeply. She had not faced what someone has called "the triple tragedy of sin, suffering, and death." When she has; when she realizes the awfulness of sin, the extent of suffering in the world, and what a robber death is as it steals our loved ones from us, she will need more than a popular magazine to help her understand life. She will need to see life through the eyes of Scripture.

People are hurting in this world. Much of their hurt is hidden behind sophisticated airs, costly cosmetics, and colorful clothes. Sometimes the hurt begins to show through tired facial muscles and sad eyes.

Even in church, people can put on a good front, but under their outward composure they may be crying out for help. They may be wrestling with doubt and want to find some answers. They may be overcome with grief and desperately needing comfort and assurance. They may be struggling with sin, and wanting to know how they can be liberated. They may be outwardly calm but inwardly in turmoil because of family problems, financial worries, problems with their work, fears about aging or failing health, or some other problem that robs them of peace of mind. They may even feel like phonies in a phony world. What book in all the world except the Bible has a message for all these groups?

The Bible is not just another book. Like no other book, it has the answer for the sin problem. It speaks to our deepest needs. We do not read the Bible for entertainment, though it does contain fascinating reading. We read it as hungry people looking for bread, as lost people looking for a way out, as persons adrift looking for a guiding star, as people in darkness looking for light, and as a signpost that points the way home. Isaiah was right when he said, "Seek and read from the book of the Lord" (Isaiah 34:16).

A Textbook for the Laboratory of Life

In his book *The Student Faces Life,* Dr. Carl Kopf said that, among other things, the Bible is a textbook in which are recorded the results of the most intensive experiments ever performed in living. It is like a class of freshmen going into a chemistry laboratory for the first time. Before them is the equipment they will use in their experiments: the beakers, the test tubes, the Bunsen burners, and the like. On a shelf above them are the chemicals. Each student is given a textbook. The teacher says, "Study the textbook. Learn the properties of each chemical. Then perform your experiments and record the results in your notebooks."

But one freshman gets rebellious. He says, "Who wants to follow the textbook all the time?" He thinks, *I wonder what would happen if I mixed some of these chemicals together?* So, when he thinks the teacher isn't looking, he begins to mix several chemicals together to see what will happen. Dr. Kopf says it happens! When the experiment comes down from the ceiling, the student doesn't have to write the result in his notebook. The stain on his notebook is the result.

One day, David experimented with faith, and the result is beautifully recorded in Psalm 23. But on another day David thought the Teacher wasn't looking, so he experimented with wife stealing and murder, and that experiment exploded on him. The stain is spread all across Chapters 11 and 12 of 2 Samuel to show that even a king can't break the laws of God without bringing suffering on himself and others.

In the case of the Bible, said Dr. Kopf, the test tube was the Mediterranean world. The chemicals were people like ourselves, Jew and Gentile. The reagents were sin and righteousness. The Bible is the precipitate for our warning, our comfort, our guidance.

Dynamite! Handle with Care!

About an hour before a president of the United States arrives to attend a church service, dogs trained to smell out explosives are led back and forth between all the pews, and into every room in the church, including the pastor's study. Any drawers that are not locked are opened, and the dogs are taken to sniff in them.

I have often jokingly said that not once during the Sundays I was privileged to preach to President and Mrs. Carter did any dog bark at my sermon notes. Evidently they felt there were no explosive ideas in what I planned to say.

Yet Paul called the gospel dynamite. In speaking of the power of the gospel, he used the Greek word *dunamis,* from which we get our word dynamite. Properly understood, the gospel is dynamite that can blow our bigotry and pride to pieces if we take its message seriously.

Often those who fear the gospel are more conscious of its explosive nature than those who profess to believe in it. Why did most of the religious leaders of Jesus' day fear him and his message so much? For one thing they realized that, if accepted, it would blow up their control of the religious life of the people. Why did some of the leaders called Judaizers fear Paul's message to the Gentile world? Because they were afraid it would blow up the idea that certain religious practices that they advocated were essential to salvation. Why did the church leaders oppose the teachings of Martin Luther? Because they recognized that his ideas were powerful enough to explode their control over the people's purse strings. Why did Hitler oppose the church? Because he knew the gospel would explode his idea of a superior race. Why does the Muslim world so fiercely oppose the preaching of the Christian message in countries under Muslim control? Because, among other things, they recognize the gospel's power to explode their outmoded ideas about the subservience of women in the home and in the world.

The gospel can explode our complacency. It can explode our prejudices. It can explode our pride. One wonders that the dogs did not react when they sniffed the Bible. It is full of explosive ideas.

Thank a Teacher

I saw it on a bumper sticker. The message began, "If you can read this . . ." I expected it to end by saying, "you are driving too close." But no, it said, "If you can read this, thank a teacher."

Habakkuk knew the importance of reading. He wanted to make his message so concise that, if it were chiseled in stone, a person could read it while running past (Habakkuk 2:2). But suppose the runner couldn't read!

Reading is one of the most important skills we can ever acquire. Imagine not being able to read a letter, a newspaper, a street sign, a traffic instruction, the destination sign on a bus, the label on a can, or anything else that calls for recognizing the written word. How handicapped we would be! What a debt we owe to those who taught us how to read!

Jesus indicated the importance of reading when he asked the lawyer, "What is written in the law? How do you read?" (Luke 10:26). But it is not only important to know *how* to read, we also must know *what* to read.

Isaiah (Isaiah 34:16), Jesus (John 5:39), and Paul (2 Timothy 3:15) all stressed the importance of reading the Bible. As no other book, it speaks to us of God.

But to be able to read, one must know the language. No matter how well one can read his native tongue, he is at a loss when it comes to reading a sign or a newspaper in a country where he does not know the language.

A cynic can read the Bible and find fault with it. But when a person approaches the Bible with the hunger to know God—when he lets the Holy Spirit be his Teacher—the Bible takes on new meaning, for then he begins to understand its language of faith and love.

Rock and Roll on Beethoven's Keyboard

In his book *Musical Laughs,* Henry T. Finck tells of a group of American tourists who visited a museum in Vienna where one of the prize exhibits was a piano that once belonged to Beethoven. A young girl in the group asked if she might play it. When she was given permission, she sat down and played a silly little tune that was popular with teenagers back in America.

The guide informed the group that Paderewski, the great Polish pianist, had visited the museum just to see that piano. When asked if he had played it, the guide said, "No. We hoped he would, but he refused. He said he wasn't worthy."

The girl is a product of our irreverent age. Nothing seems sacred anymore. Millions take their cue from Hollywood instead of the Bible. Nothing seems to move them to reverential awe. There are even those who would malign Jesus.

To reverence something does not mean to make an idol of it. A minister held a Bible in his hand as he preached. A parishioner later said, "Did you notice how tenderly he caressed the Bible as he spoke?" But God doesn't want us to caress the Bible. He wants us to read it and live by it. We should approach its message with reverence and awe, for it, as no other book, contains the Word of God.

The world has gone hog-wild away from God's Word. Think how sex has been dragged down into the mud. When the same thing happened in Corinth, God didn't blast the city with a thunderbolt. He just gave up on some of the people (Romans 1:24). What a judgment! They did not defile sex. They defiled themselves. People don't hurt the Bible when they scorn it. It has been scorned before. They hurt themselves.

What Time Is It?

In a small industrial town, a certain man called the telephone operator every morning to ask for the correct time. After this had gone on for quite a long time, the operator asked him why he called to ask for the time every morning. "Because," he explained, "I blow the whistle at the mill, and I want to be sure I have the right time."

The man heard a little gasp. "What's the matter?" he asked. The telephone operator said, "Ever since you started calling to ask for the time, I have been setting my watch by that whistle."

They had been relying on each other for the correct time. What they needed was to be in touch with a scientific instrument that could determine the correct time by the movement of the stars.

So often we set our standards by one another. We copy each other in so many ways—in our attitudes, our prejudices, our standards of right and wrong. We need a standard beyond ourselves, one that can lift us above human error.

Fortunately, the Bible gives us such a standard. For one thing, it gives us the Ten Commandments. Who can improve on them? As someone has said, we don't break them, we break ourselves against them. They are like gravity. It doesn't prevent us from jumping off a tall building, but it determines that we will fall if we do.

Yet Jesus did improve on the Ten Commandments. He said, "It has been said . . . but I say unto you." He made God's love the standard. "You, therefore, must be perfect, as your heavenly Father is perfect" (Matthew 5:48).

We need biblical guidance. What time is it? The Bible may say, "It is time to seek God's forgiveness," or "It is time to forgive," or "It is time to take a stand," or "It is time to show someone you care."

Time is ticking away. None of us knows how much of it he has left. We need to check our lives not against human standards but against God's.

Who Are We?

About five miles east of Auburn, Maine, there is an old historic church building called the Penley Corner Church. The state declared it to be a historic landmark and contributed funds to have it restored to its original condition.

Only one service a year is now held in the old building. People from all over the area come to that annual service. For several years I have been asked to deliver the sermon at that service. After one of these events I talked to a man who had not met me before. After I had asked him who he was, he asked me, "And who are you?"

This is one of the most important questions we can ask. Who are we, anyhow? Obviously, we are physical beings with all the hungers and limitations of the flesh. Obviously, too, those hungers must be controlled, lest they lead to gluttony and lust.

But we are more. We are psychological beings. We have hungers that bread and butter can't satisfy, such as the hunger for fulfillment. We are social beings. We seek the company of others. We crave acceptance. Furthermore, we are intelligent beings. We have minds. We can think.

Some people would stop there. Communism, for example, sees nothing beyond the grave. It sees persons merely as creatures of the state who have only those rights and privileges the state permits them to have.

But the Bible doesn't stop there. It says we are spiritual beings made in the image of God. As such, we have rights that even the state should recognize and protect, such as the right to worship.

Not only that, but the Bible says two things more. It says we are sinners, and as such we stand condemned before the righteousness of God. But we also are people for whom Christ died. Nothing reveals our worth in the sight of God more than that. God considers us worth the price paid for our redemption on Calvary.

11

The Living Witness of the Church

John 14:12 just has to be one of the most incredible statements in the Bible. And yet it is the promise of Jesus: "Truly, truly I say to you, he who believes in me will also do the works that I do; *and greater works than these will he do,* because I go to my Father."

Greater works than Jesus did? Greater works than he who turned water into wine? Greater works than he who healed the sick and opened the eyes of the blind? Greater works than he who stilled the storm with his voice and raised the dead?

Incredible! Impossible!

And yet Jesus said it.

And the miracle is happening.

I don't think he meant that you or I will do these things individually. But, when we join our faith, our loyalty, our prayers, our talents, our stewardship with others in churches, and when churches join together in larger groups of churches, we are able to help build schools, hospitals, mission centers, and other forms of Christian ministry that can teach more people every day, bring a healing ministry to more sick people every day, feed more hungry people every day, bring love and caring to more lonely and distraught people every day than Jesus was able to touch in his entire lifetime.

We don't perform the miracle. God does that. God heals the sick, forgives the sinful, comforts the weary, gives peace to those who sorrow, and hope to those who despair. God gives love to those who feel forsaken. Yet God works through us. God gives us intelligence and skills by which we provide churches, schools, hospitals, mission stations for divine use, just as a boy's lunch once helped Jesus to feed the multitude.

Not only do we need churches to get the work of the kingdom done, but they give individual Christians the encouragement and support which can only come from a larger group. The author of Ecclesiastes spoke wisely when he wrote, "Two are better than one, because they have a good reward for their toil. . . . A threefold cord

114

is not quickly broken'' (Ecclesiastes 4:9, 12). When the world throws temptation at us or scoffs at our faith and ideals, our assurance that hosts of people in the churches are behind us can give us courage to take a stand and to maintain a Christian witness. We gain new courage when we know we are not alone in our convictions.

If there were no churches, we would have to invent something like them to provide worship, fellowship, and opportunities for broader Christian service. Let us look, then, at some illustrations of God's truth as they are brought to light by the work and witness of the churches.

Indoors/Outdoors

In the last years of his life, William Wordsworth, the famous English poet, lived in a home called Rydal Mount near Grasmere, England. The setting is unforgettably beautiful, with surrounding mountains and nearby Lake Windermere.

A servant there once said to a visitor, "This is my master's library where he keeps his books; his study is out-of-doors."

Wordsworth drew much of his inspiration from nature. Indoors, he thought of a world of "getting and spending" where people "lay waste their powers." Outdoors, his spirit was renewed by the sight of a "host of golden daffodils." Indoors, he was bound by four walls and a ceiling. Outdoors, he could walk in his garden, look at the mountains, or walk along the lake.

Yet he needed the indoors, too. He needed its protection from the elements. Indoors, he could control the temperature. Outdoors, he was at the mercy of heat and cold, wind and rain.

We need both. Some people say they can worship God better outdoors than in any church. Certainly we need the out-of-doors with its reminder of God's creative powers and bounty toward us, but we need the church, too. We need its symbolic reminders of the faith. We need the contagion of worshiping with other seekers after God. We need to join with them to see that Christian truths and ideals are perpetuated. The out-of-doors can remind us of the creative power of God, but we also need the church with its continuing call for commitment to the way of the cross.

Monument or Ministry?

I don't think he meant to say it the way he did, for he had enjoyed an effective ministry there. But, writing about a church he had served, a former pastor wrote, "It proudly stands as a monument to the faithfulness of God."

Monument! Is that what he meant to say? How much better if he had said, "The church stands as a *living witness* to the faithfulness of God."

That's just the trouble! Too many churches have become little more than monuments to their former zeal. Once these churches had a magnetic fellowship and bore an effective witness to Christian faith. But now, except for the faithfulness of a few, the zeal of former days has departed. The worship is dull. Prayers are perfunctory. Conversions are few. The Bible is more praised than studied. Outreach to the community has become nil. As with Samson, the power of the Lord seems to have departed from them (Judges 16:20).

Pride of the past can never be a substitute for power in the present. Often a changing community can cause a church to lose members as people move from the area. But, as long as it stands, people should know that there they can find compassion; there they can find a genuine love for God; there they can find a genuine zeal for the Christian cause.

Monuments have their place as reminders of the past, but churches are meant to be living witnesses to the power of God in the present. Happy the church that refuses to become a monument as it seeks to minister in the name of Christ.

Wholehearted or Halfhearted?

Once when Thomas Edison looked tired, his wife suggested that they take a vacation. "Think where you'd rather go than any other place in all the world," she is reported to have said, "and let's go there." A short time later, she asked him, "Have you thought where you'd most like to go?" "Yes," he replied, "to my laboratory."

Dean Hole felt the same way about growing roses. In a book called *A Book About Roses* published in 1869, he wrote: "He who would have beautiful roses in his garden must have beautiful roses in his heart. He must love them well and always. To win, he must woo them as Jacob wooed Laban's daughter, though drought and frost consume. He must have not only the glowing admiration, the enthusiasm, and the passion, but the tenderness, the thoughtfulness, the reverence, the watchfulness of love."

That's the way the early followers felt about Jesus. They gladly left all to follow him. But as people got farther away from the days of his earthly ministry, the ardor of many began to cool. Some, like Demas, forsook him altogether. Others, like many in the church in Laodicea, became lukewarm (Revelation 3:14-16)—not cold, just lukewarm, but, so far as bearing an effective witness for Christ was concerned, they might just as well have been cold.

Halfhearted Christians—that's the trouble with the church in America. Not persecution, not out-and-out rejection, just half-hearted support. Once again, one hears the cry, "Would that you were cold or hot!" (Revelation 3:15).

A halfhearted inventor would never have invented the electric light. A halfhearted gardener will never create a beautiful rose garden. Halfhearted Christians will never create a triumphant church. They must be, as the hymn puts it, "truehearted, wholehearted, faithful and loyal."

What's Your Label?

A certain minister served as an interim pastor in a Maryland church. The people found him to be a person who really enjoyed life and his religion. When his ministry there came to an end, the congregation gave a party for him. Along with other gifts, they showered him with canned goods but, as a practical joke, they first removed the labels from the cans. He could not tell by looking at them what they contained. One can imagine the amused frustration he and his wife must have felt when they opened the cans to see how they could use the contents in the meal they were preparing.

Sometimes labels can be disconcerting. We all are too prone to label a person "conservative" or "liberal," "native" or "foreigner," "Catholic" or "Protestant," and so on, and then to judge the person by that label. How tragic it is if we fail to see the real person behind the label!

Labels do serve a purpose, though. They help to identify who we are. How proudly we should wear the label of our work, our nationality, and our religious faith!

Paul was not ashamed to be labeled as a follower of Jesus. The label "Christian" is one that everyone should be glad to wear, not in a better-than-thou attitude but in grateful recognition that through faith in Christ we have found peace with God.

"Church member" is another label we should be proud to wear. Some people would argue that a person can be a Christian without joining a church. Perhaps so, but he would be somewhat like a can without a label. To refuse to wear a denominational label may be the sign of a liberal spirit, but it may also be a cop-out for those who are unwilling to get involved in Christian work.

What label most represents the real you? Paul proudly wore the label "apostle." Can we wear the label "disciple" as proudly?

Wanted—Fence Movers

There is a beautiful story that came out of World War I. An American Protestant chaplain stationed in Italy became a friend of a Roman Catholic priest. The chaplain moved on with his unit and was killed. When the priest heard of his death, he asked if the body could be buried in the little cemetery by his church.

The military authorities gave permission, but the priest ran into an unexpected problem. Church officials felt they could not give approval for a non-Catholic to be buried in consecrated soil. So the priest buried his friend just outside the fence.

Years later, an American who had known of the situation visited the old priest and asked to see the chaplain's grave. To his surprise, the grave was inside the fence. "Oh," he said, "You got permission to move the body." "No," replied the priest. "They just told me where I couldn't bury the body. No one ever told me I couldn't move the fence."

No less a person than Pope John XXIII began to move some fences. It was he who began the long process of bringing Protestants and Catholics closer together. Too long fences of dogma have divided fellow Christians, but there are ways of moving these fences. Many Christians are discovering how to maintain their denominational identity and yet demonstrate to the world their oneness with all who are sincere followers of Christ.

Someone has pointed out that the barriers that divide us as Christians are not made of stone and mortar, which could be knocked down with a bulldozer. They are more like walls of mist that can only be dissipated by sunshine.

Fortunately, many today are feeling the warmth of Christ's love in such a way as to dissipate their intolerance of others. There are still, however, many misunderstandings and antagonisms left in the world. The world today can still use some more fence movers.

On Cutting Off Both Ends of a Ham

A young bride in the country received a ham from a friend. Before putting it in the oven to bake, she cut off a piece from both ends of the ham. Her husband asked her why she did it. She replied, "I don't know, but mother always did." So later he asked his mother-in-law, "Do you always cut off both ends of a ham before you bake it?" She replied, "Oh yes, I always do." "Why?" asked her son-in-law. "I don't know," she replied, "but mother always did." Still later, he asked the grandmother, "Do you always cut off both ends of a ham before you bake it?" "Oh, yes," she said, "I always do." "But why?" he asked. "Because I can't make it fit into my pan if I don't," was the reply.

This is the way traditions get started. Regarding some of the religious practices of their day, some leaders were concerned with when and how they were done. Jesus was interested not in how but in why. Others were concerned that rituals be observed at stated times and in a prescribed manner. Jesus was interested that they be done in the right spirit and from the right motive.

Traditional practices have their place. Youth is wrong if it wants to discard them all. The traditions of wearing a wedding ring, of shaking hands when we meet, of closing our eyes to shut out distractions when we pray—all these are meaningful if they do not cover up hypocrisy. On the other hand, if a tradition loses its meaning, we should not be afraid to discard it.

Someone has said that the seven last words of the church are "we never did it that way before." The church that is unwilling to change, that relies wholly on the past without developing innovative ideas for the present, is apt to be on its way out. It must learn how to keep its link with the past and yet serve the present and look toward the future.

Gray and White

For many years until his death, Dr. Oscar Blackwelder was the greatly beloved pastor of the Church of the Reformation in Washington, D. C. The church is located just a block and a half east of the United States Capitol and just around the corner from the Supreme Court.

Dr. Blackwelder used to like to make this observation: The marble of which the Supreme Court building is built appears so white that under the summer sun, it fairly blinds one to look at it. When it snows, however, the Supreme Court building looks gray by comparison.

When we compare ourselves to others, we usually manage to come off pretty well. We can always find someone with whom it is safe to compare ourselves. We can say, "I'm not like that old hypocrite, or that old skinflint"—in which case our pride becomes as offensive as the other person's hypocrisy or miserliness. But when we compare ourselves to Christ, or to the person God wants us to be, we come out at a different evaluation.

Someone has said, "If thou couldst see the person God made, thou nevermore couldst be the person thou art, content." In other words, who begins to live up to what God expects of him or her? The dark glasses of self-conceit cannot hide the whiteness of God's expectations for us, especially as those expectations were made visible in Christ.

So you who are in the church, don't go placing yourself above those outside the church. You are just fortunate enough to have welcomed God's grace and to know that you need the church to help you become a better person. You who are outside the church, don't try to exalt yourself above the hypocrites in the church. At least they are there because they are willing to admit they need God's help and the help of the church. Your arrogance can be as offensive in God's sight as their failure to live up more perfectly to the Christian ideal.

Folds and a Flock

Dr. Donald Barnhouse, for many years an eminent Philadelphia clergyman, used to say, "The Bible says we are brothers and sisters in Christ, but nowhere does it say we are identical twins."

Jesus once said, "I have other sheep, that are not of this fold; I must bring them also . . . so there shall be one flock, one shepherd" (John 10:16).

In reporting Jesus' words, John uses two different Greek words: *aule* and *poimne*. So that the verse reads, "I have other sheep that are not of this *aule;* I must bring them also . . . so there will be one *poimne*, one shepherd."

Obviously the meaning of the two words is not completely identical. Yet the King James Version translated both of these words by the one English word "fold." William Barclay says this tempts some Christians to say, "See, there is only one fold—one church—and we are it." But most present-day Greek scholars, including the Revised Standard translators, agree that the second word means "flock." A wealthy sheep owner could have several folds, but all the sheep in all his folds go to make his flock.

So there can be a Methodist fold, a Baptist fold, a Catholic fold, a Nazarene fold, and so on, but if the sheep in these folds are loyal to the one true Shepherd, they are part of his flock.

Christians do not impress the world by uniformity but by evidences of unity in spite of their differences.

Help for the Bleeding

Dr. Edward Bauman tells about some Boy Scouts who were learning first aid. Three of them, who were to pretend they needed medical attention, were stationed along a trail. As they came to each of these, the others were to administer the necessary aid. The third scout was to pretend to have a severe cut with much bleeding. But the boys took so long in ministering to the first two that the third one got tired of waiting. When the other scouts arrived at the place where he had been stationed, they found a note that said, "I have bled to death, and gone home."

Millions of people must feel that way about the church. They were hungry, but no one came to feed them; thirsty, but no one gave them something to drink; strangers, but no one came to welcome them; naked, but no one gave them any clothes; sick or in prison, but no one came to comfort them. So they have gone off to the world to get the attention they desire.

The world is full of people who are still waiting to hear God's word of hope and salvation. Sometimes the church gets so busy ministering to its own needs that it never gets around to ministering to those who are still waiting for some evidence of God's love—to those who, spiritually speaking, are bleeding to death.

Of course, the task is too great for any one Christian or church or denomination to do it alone. But if each Christian told one other person about Christ; if each Christian would seek out at least one other person to whom to offer some evidence of caring; if each Christian would give what he or she can to support the missionary outreach of his or her church, the church would go a long way toward meeting the need.

12
The Joy of Stewardship

If churches did nothing else to justify their existence, they still would render a valuable service by encouraging people to give voluntarily, and even sacrificially, for the sake of others. Take away voluntary giving, and churches would cease to exist. Schools, hospitals, missionary activities, in fact all forms of ministry founded and operated by churches, would cease to exist. Take away the training in stewardship provided by the churches, and the world would lose its finest example of voluntary and sacrificial giving.

For Christians, giving is tied to the purposes of God as expressed in the ministry and outreach of the churches. Several years ago, the treasurer of a large denomination managed to steal almost two million dollars of the denomination's funds. Church leaders were forced to borrow heavily to finance the Christian activities that would have been supported by the stolen money.

Certain bank officials suggested that the churches declare a moratorium on all missionary activity until the loan was repaid. One of the church officials said, "If you ask us to do that, you'll never get your money, for you will take away our very reason for being. Let us continue with the mission for which Christ himself has commissioned us, and you'll get your money." And they did.

The Bible is very clear in its call for giving. One of the Old Testament prophets went so far as to suggest that to fail to give a certain percentage of one's possessions for the sake of God's work is actually to rob God of that which rightfully belongs to God (Malachi 3:8-10). Jesus urged his followers to give, promising them rich spiritual blessings in return (Luke 6:38). The apostle Paul urged Christians to give for God's work, not in a grudging spirit but with a grateful and cheerful heart (2 Corinthians 9:7).

The miracle is that so many people give so much of their hard-earned money for the sake of God's kingdom. Their reward is not only in seeing God's work strengthened in the world but also in discovering the joy and satisfaction that giving for worthwhile causes can bring to the giver.

Even so, most Christians need to be challenged to be better stewards of that which God has enabled them to possess. Most people would be embarrassed to eat in a first-class restaurant and leave a tip of less than ten or fifteen percent of the bill. Yet, after filling their own needs and desires, most Christians give what amounts to a much smaller tip than that to the Lord. God deserves better than that.

God wants our stewardship not as a fee which we would pay to belong to a country club but as an expression of our realization and acceptance of God's ownership of all things. God wants our stewardship as an expression of our gratitude for all the blessings God has given us. God wants our stewardship as our indication of wanting to share in trying to make this a better world.

The following illustrations seek to give us some glimpses of stewardship which may help others to catch glimpses of God's truth and love.

From Sty to Throne

Shakespeare once asked, "What's in a name?" Sometimes it's more than meets the eye. Take the word "steward," for example. Originally it came from two old-English words "sty" and "wart" or "ward." A sty-wart or sty-ward was a person who looked after the animals on a rich man's estate. In time, it came to mean the person who managed the entire estate.

Still later it became a family name. Sometimes it was spelled Stewart or Steward. In fact, one family bearing this name became the ruling family of England. Tradition has it that Mary Queen of Scots changed the spelling to Stuart because the French pronounced Stewart as if it were spelled Ste-var.

That is quite a climb for a word—all the way from an animal pen to a monarch's throne. It reminds us that God wants us to lift our stewardship above the level of an unpleasant duty to where we enthrone it as a privilege in our lives.

A stewart or steward did not own the estate he managed. He managed it as a trusted servant of its owner. This is the basic principle of stewardship. It begins by recognizing God's overall ownership (Psalm 50:10). We are entrusted with God's estate for a time, so we must recognize our responsibility to care for it as stewards.

The air is ours to breathe, not to pollute. The water is ours to drink, not to make impure. The raw materials of earth are ours to use, not to use up. As stewards of God, we must treat God's earth with respect and remember our responsibility to future generations. We must not treat the earth as a pigpen, but as part of God's throne.

Our lives are God's also. God wants us to love God so much that stewardship ceases to be a burden and becomes a way of showing gratitude for the privilege of working with God.

When Franklin Heard Whitefield

Benjamin Franklin once went to hear the great evangelist George Whitefield. In his autobiography he tells us what happened:

"I happened soon after to attend one of his sermons, in the course of which, I perceived he intended to finish with a collection, and I silently resolved he should get nothing from me. I had in my pocket a handful of copper money, three or four silver dollars, and five pistoles of gold. As he proceeded, I began to soften, and concluded to give the coppers. Another stroke of his oratory made me ashamed of that, and determined me to give the silver. And he finished so admirably that I emptied my pocket wholly into the collection dish, gold and all."

Every preacher might wish he could preach like that. Few, however, can match the eloquence of a Whitefield. Our stewardship, therefore,—what we think about and do with our life and possessions—should not be based on someone's oratory, nor should it consist in an occasional emptying of one's purse. It should be based on the recognition that all things—our life and the planet on which we live it, the air we breathe and the ability to breathe it—everything comes from God. In everything, therefore, we are to be stewards for God, and whether we spend time, energy, thought, or money, we should glorify God in all that we think and do.

It is not just that a tenth of what we possess belongs to God, and the rest is ours to do with as we please. Everything belongs to God. God expects us to spend all of it in accordance with God's will. God knows we must spend much of it for our own needs (Matthew 6:31-32), but God expects us to spend some (the Bible suggests at least a tenth) for the work of God's kingdom and the welfare of others.

Keeping What We Give Away

When the late Clifford McIntire was a congressman from Maine, he visited a country fair where there was a contest to see whose team or yoke of oxen could pull the heaviest load. After the contest was over, the congressman went to see the owner of the winning team.

"How many yoke of oxen do you own?" asked Mr. McIntire. The owner of the winning pair replied, "Ten." "Isn't that a lot of oxen for one person to own?" asked the congressman. With dry humor, the owner replied, "Some people go to Florida."

In other words, a person can do what he chooses to do with his money. What appeals to one person may not appeal to another. A person tends to put his money where his interests lie.

But our money is not ours to spend thoughtlessly. In a very real sense, it is God's money, too. God gave us the raw materials of the earth. God gave us our health and our ability to earn money. God wants us to think of God when we spend it. God wants us to treat all our money as a trust and to use some of it in the service of the kingdom.

On the wall of the student center of Georgetown College in Georgetown, Kentucky, there is a tribute to the donor. First there is his name, Lee E. Cralle, Jr., and then the date of his gift, October 16, 1965. Then follows this statement: "That which a man gives away often becomes his greatest possession."

Russell H. Conwell raised over two million dollars with his famous lecture "Acres of Diamonds," but he gave it all away in scholarships for needy young people, and in helping to establish Temple University and Good Samaritan Hospital (now a part of Temple Medical School in Philadelphia). Dr. Conwell was never wealthy, but he was rich in the gratitude of thousands who benefitted from his generosity.

Oxen and Florida have their appeal for some people, but he who spends his money *only* for selfish interests ends up poor indeed.

A Cheerful (?) Giver

Dr. W. O. Lewis used to tell about a man who went to church with a one-dollar bill and a ten-dollar bill in his pocket. This was back in the days when a dollar was much more valuable than it is now. He intended to put the one-dollar bill in the offering, but after church he discovered that he had made a mistake, and had put the ten-dollar bill in the offering plate instead. After thinking about it, he shrugged, and said, "Oh well, God will give me credit for making a ten-dollar contribution." "No, he won't," said Dr. Lewis, "he will give you credit for one dollar, for that's what you intended to give."

A small amount given in love, is worth more in the sight of God than a large amount given grudgingly or by mistake. That principle doesn't mean we should give pennies when we can afford to give dollars. It does mean that, whatever the gift, it should come from a sincere and loving heart.

Jesus was interested in what people gave. He stood in the temple and watched people as they put their money in the treasury box. Some put in a large gift with a flourish. A poor widow came by and quietly dropped in two pennies. This was the gift that thrilled Jesus. The wealthy would not miss what they gave, but the widow gave her food money. It was more important to her to give to the Lord than it was to have enough food on her table.

Of course, we do not have to be poor to make our gifts count. Whatever the state of our finances, we should put real thought and love in what we give and do for others and for God. It's not the size of the gift that counts, but the love it represents and the resources from which we give it.

Mary's gift was not small when she poured spikenard on Jesus' feet (John 12:3-7). It was expensive. It was even extravagant, and the disciples were shocked. But Jesus welcomed it as an evidence of genuine love. This was no calculated effort to win his approval. It was a selfless outpouring of gratitude and love.

What Do Your Check Stubs Say?

When Philip Guedalla set out to write a biography of the Duke of Wellington, he wondered how he could find out what the duke was really like. Research in libraries could tell where he went and what he did, but what kind of a person was he? What were his priorities? his primary interests? What came first in his life?

Then one day the biographer chanced upon something he felt would give him a clue. He found a bunch of the duke's check stubs. By studying these the author could discover what the great Englishman really put first in his life, what his chief interests really were.

What would others think of us if they examined our check stubs? What could we learn about ourselves if we seriously studied our check stubs for the past year? How much have we spent over and above the necessities of life, and for what? How much have we spent for luxuries and pleasures? How much, if anything, have we given to worthwhile causes and for those in dire need? How much have we given for the cause of Christ? Did a share for Christ's work come first, or did we give him something from what was left over after we had paid all other expenses?

It may not have occurred to us, but when we write our checks, in a sense we are writing the story of our life. We are revealing how materialistic or pleasure-loving we really are; how much we are committed to the cause of Christ; how sensitive we are to the needs of others.

Spared for What?

During World War I, when Dr. George W. Truett was pastor of the First Baptist Church of Dallas, a young man who was a member of his church was crippled in the war. Later he received forty thousand dollars for his injuries (an amount worth at least ten times that much today).

Upon receiving the money, the young man went to see Dr. Truett and gave him a check for four thousand dollars, a tithe of what he had received, for the work of the church. Dr. Truett was very reluctant to accept it. He pointed out that the young man's earning capacity would undoubtedly be lessened, and he would probably need the money for himself.

The young man explained, "You don't understand. I saw some of my buddies blown to bits. I was lucky. I'm still alive. My life was spared. I don't know why I was spared and others were not. I have decided that God must have spared my life for a reason, and what better reason could there be than to help him with his work?"

When tragedy strikes many people are tempted to ask, "Why has this happened to me?" But there is another question that most people need to ask: "Why have I been spared the tragedy that has come to others?"

Some have physical handicaps, but most of us are spared. Why are we spared, if not to do what we can to help others who are less fortunate than we are? Some of our peers have died. Why have we been spared, if not to do what we can to help make this a better world? Others may have little to give, but we may have been blessed in what we possess. Why, if not to share some of our blessings for the sake of others, and to help God do work in the world?

About Cows and Contributions

Dr. Earle V. Pierce used to tell about a city man who moved to the country and bought a cow to provide milk for his table. In a short time, his cow went dry and he was obliged to go to a neighboring farmer to see if he could arrange to buy milk.

"But that cow has not been fresh very long," said the farmer. "I'm surprised it has gone dry so soon." "I am surprised too," said the city man, "for I have certainly been considerate of that animal. If I didn't need any milk, I didn't milk her. If I only needed a quart, I only took a quart."

"The way to keep milk coming from a cow," Dr. Pierce used to point out, "is not to take as little as possible, but as much as the cow can give. The way to keep streams of joy flowing in the Christian life," he would add, "is not to give as little as possible, but as much as we can according to how God has blessed us."

The minister who seeks to protect his people from giving is not doing them a service. He is depriving them of one of the best ways to deepen their Christian loyalty.

We don't lose interest in a company by investing in it. Nor do we lose interest in the church by giving to it. Just the opposite! When we invest or give money, our concern increases. It was Jesus himself who reminded us that where we invest our life and our means is where our interest is most apt to be stimulated and grow. Sacrificial giving can sometimes do more than prayer or Bible study to increase our interest in the Lord's work.

13

The Challenge to Reach Out

I once started to study Hebrew with a Jewish rabbi friend of mine. In the Hebrew language there is a word that is known as the ineffable name for God. It is so sacred that a devout Jew will never pronounce it out loud; it is too sacred to be taken on human lips. Instead of pronouncing the name the way it is written, my friend instructed me to say *Adonai,* meaning "Jehovah" or "Master." I later learned that an orthodox Jew will not even pronounce this word, but will say a word like *Shekanyah,* meaning "the One who dwells with us," instead.

One day as I was reading a passage in Hebrew, I came to the ineffable name for God. And I forgot what the rabbi had told me. I didn't say *Adonai* or *Shekanyah;* I said the word the way it was written. My rabbi friend shouted, "NO!" Then he said, "Please, that is the ineffable name for God. It is too sacred to be taken on human lips. Please say *Adonai* instead."

I apologized. I would not willingly offend him or his religious convictions. I promised I would never pronounce the ineffable name for God out loud again, and I have kept my promise. In a world where there is so little reverence toward everything sacred, it is comforting to know there is this much reverence left for the name of God. I wish some of my Christian friends had something of this same reverence for the name of God and of God's son, Jesus Christ, so that when they spoke these names they would do so in utter reverence.

"But," I said to my friend, "would you not agree that a better way to do honor to the name of God is not just to refrain from saying a particular word, but to live a godly life? After all, the Psalmist says, 'He leadeth me in the paths of righteousness for his name's sake.' That is what really does honor to the name of God—to walk in paths of righteousness."

And he agreed.

In a similar way, as one of the New Testament writers reminds us, what good would it do to say we hold God in reverence if we despise our brother who also is beloved of God (1 John 4:20)?

In a sense, one cannot be Christian alone. One must be Christian toward someone. Of course, Christian impulses must begin within a person, but one's feelings can only be made evident by the way that individual relates to his or her neighbor as well as to God.

Someone has said you cannot measure Christianity with just a plumb line. You must use a try square, which enables a person to verify a right angle. There must be a vertical line between God and the believer. There must also be a horizontal line between the believer and other people.

Think how Jesus taught us to pray: "Forgive us our debts." There you have the line between God and the one who prays. "As we forgive our debtors." There you have the qualifying line between the person and others.

Or again, "God is able to provide you with every blessing in abundance [the line between God and the believer] so that you may always have enough of everything and may provide in abundance for every good work [the line between the believer and others]" (2 Corinthians 9:8).

One's confession must be matched by one's character.

One's profession must be matched by one's performance.

One's upreach must be matched by one's outreach.

One's claim of inner grace must be matched by one's outward show of goodness toward others.

Both Inside and Outside

When Queen Victoria lived in Buckingham Palace, according to biographer Cecil Woodham-Smith, the maintenance of the outside of the palace was under the supervision of the Office of Woods and Forests, while the maintenance of the inside was under the supervision of the Lord Chamberlain and his staff. This meant that one group was responsible for washing the outside of the windows and another for the inside. When these two groups failed to work together, the queen, says her biographer, had to look "through obscured and dirty windows."

Sometimes Christians are like that. They claim to let God deal with their inner lives, but they let the world dictate their business ethics and their social behavior. Thus, they look at life through dirty windows, for a window that is washed on only one side is still dirty.

As Jesus reminds us, we cannot serve God with our inner lives and mammon with our outer lives. Christ must be in control of both. He must guide us in our work as well as in our worship, in our pleasures as well as in our prayers. We must try to be as Christian in the way we seek our pleasures and deal with others as we try to be when we go to church. It must be clear to others that Christ controls our ethics as well as our emotions, our morals as well as our meditations. Like Zacchaeus, who returned fourfold the money he had taken dishonestly, we must give convincing evidence by our outward dealings that we have really experienced a change of heart.

Message from a Granite Quarry

Outside the city of Barre, Vermont, is the largest granite quarry in the world. It is known as the "Rock of Ages" quarry, and its granite is used for fine tombstones and monuments all over the world. The quarry measures forty acres at the surface and more than 350 feet deep. Workers are lowered into it by an elevator bucket, and they look small indeed from the rim of the quarry.

One day I stood with a representative of the company looking down into the quarry. "My," I remarked, "you have a deep hole here." "Yes," he agreed, "we have gone as deep as we can go without going wider." "What do you mean?" I asked. He explained, "Though the walls are granite, the pressure of the surrounding earth is so great that if we went much deeper without going wider, we might have a cave-in."

So often in our religious life we want a deeper awareness of God. We pray, "O God, give us a deepened sense of thy presence." But sometimes God must feel like saying, "You have gone as deep as you can without going wider. Reach out to those around you. Ask what you can do to help, to show that you care. Find out how you can identify with those who cry out for justice. In so doing you may be made more aware of your own dependence upon divine guidance. In this way your own faith may be deepened."

In these days when the surrounding pressures of social change are so great, if the church does not widen its outreach of service to others, it may face a cave-in of criticism and reproach, and find its influence buried under the weight of community indifference. Granite is not quarried to be stored away but to be used in the world. Christ's love is not given us to store, but to share.

Incident in Hong Kong

The gifted preacher Dr. Vernon Richardson once told me this incident. He was walking down a street in Hong Kong when he noticed a thin little Chinese girl on the sidewalk. She was kneeling with her head against the window of a bakery. She had evidently knelt there so long that she had gone to sleep in that position. It was such a touching sight that Vernon stopped and took her picture.

When he returned to the University Baptist Church in Baltimore, where he was then the pastor, he showed the pictures of his trip. Commenting on the picture of the little girl, one member asked, "What did you do after you took the picture?"

Dr. Richardson replied, "What can I say? I am ashamed to admit that I didn't wake her up to see if she was hungry, as she probably was. I didn't buy her a loaf of bread. I just went on my way photographing more need."

Do we not do the same? We read of world hunger. Our hearts are stirred by pictures of sad-eyed, thin-limbed children who bear the marks of hunger on their bodies. But what do we do after we have seen the pictures?

One loaf of bread, one contribution, won't solve the problem, but at least it's something. The problem must be attacked on a broader front. In the long run, political and economic problems that cause hunger must be solved. But starving people can't wait. They need food now.

Jesus drew the picture. He spoke of those who are hungry, thirsty, lonely, naked, in prison (Matthew 25:35-36). Are we doing anything to help change the picture?

The Other Fellow

Many years ago, before warnings could be sent out by radio, a hurricane swept across Salem harbor. Anxious residents gathered on the shore to watch as fishing boats made their way back to the shore. Through the storm people could see that one of the boats had capsized, and a fisherman could be seen clinging to it.

Five men got into a small boat to go out to rescue the fisherman. The mother of one of the men said, "Son, you can't go out there. It's too dangerous." The son replied, "But, Mother, you always taught us to put the other fellow first," and he went out to rescue the drowning man. Only when he reached him did he discover it was his own brother, who neither he nor his mother had known had taken out one of the fishing boats that day.

Dr. E. Stanley Jones used to say there are three levels at which we may relate ourselves to other people. We can say, "I am my brother's superior. It is up to me to maintain my position. It is up to him to keep his place." What a lot of tragedy has resulted because so many have lived at that level!

At a higher level we say, "I am my brother's keeper." In this complex, interrelated world we help one another whether we want to or not. But it is possible to help another without really loving that person.

The highest level is reached when we are willing to say, "The other fellow is my brother." We are all created by the same God. When we hate and when we quarrel with one another, it hurts the God who created us all. What a difference it could make if we would remember that the other person is equally the object of God's love and concern!

Pharisees Old and New

A youth named Don de Young was sent as a home missionary to East Harlem. He found sin, and plenty of it. But he also found evidences of sacrifice, loyalty, and love. He wrote,

> Soon after my arrival in East Harlem in July, 1955, I discovered that my evangelical mission training had betrayed me. I had been taught that the object of my mission was deprived. The other guy needed me, and I could help him. Romantic notions of the good Samaritan and self-indulging philanthropy became the basis of a crippling fiction. I had been commissioned as a "missionary" to work in East Harlem. Light meeting darkness, goodness meeting evil, the helpful meeting the helpless—this is how I was commissioned for meeting the deprived. But suddenly I discovered that I too was deprived! That is what I mean by feeling betrayed. Why had I not learned about this deficiency? The promotional materials were so anxious to fix me as the "good guy" that a spiritual superiority became a pious perversion.[1]

Not all Pharisees lived in Jesus' day. Many are alive today. Pharisees thought of themselves as being better than other people, just as some Christians today think they are a cut above people who belong to a different church, or who are non-Christians. They forget they themselves are sinners, too, who have been reached by God's grace.

In some ways the Pharisees *were* better than other people, but they took all the credit. They took such pride in their religious loyalty that they squeezed all the love out of it. Religion for them had become a servile obedience to rules and practices, not a joyous sharing of God's love with others.

[1]*Christianity Today,* June 10, 1966.

Jumble of Links or Chain of Service?

A man was walking along the street pulling a chain after him. "Why are you pulling that chain?" someone asked him. "Did you ever try to push one?" the man replied.

People are a lot like links in a chain. They can be led, but they cannot be pushed against their will.

The world of Jesus' day was full of pushers—the Caesars and centurions, for example. When they spoke, people had to jump. Jesus characterized them by saying, "You know that the rulers of the Gentiles lord it over them" (Matthew 20:25). But Jesus wanted his followers to be different: "Whoever would be great among you must be your servant . . ." (Matthew 20:26).

In his book *The Social Principles of Jesus,* Walter Rauschenbusch asked why Jesus chose the persons he did to be his disciples. They were not theologically trained. They were not men of affluence or authority. They were, on the surface at least, quite ordinary. One answer, he suggested, is that Jesus wanted to introduce a new kind of leadership into the world—a leadership that would serve and not exploit—and he chose people who were not spoiled by the possession of power.

Many people in Jesus' time thought of leadership as climbing on top of people to a position of authority and power. Jesus thought of leadership as getting underneath people and their problems, and trying to lift them to a new life and hope. He himself would set the example, "Even as the Son of man came not to be served but to serve, and to give his life a ransom for many" (Matthew 20:28).

We are called to be pullers, not pushers; lifters, not oppressors; persuaders, not dictators; compassionate, not arrogant.

Thanks, Mom. Thanks, Dad.

I was a freshman in college at the time. My roommate and I had decided to go downtown after my last class. When I came into the room, he was writing a letter. "I want to finish this before I go," he said. "Next Sunday is Mother's Day, and I'm writing to tell my mother I love her."

When he finished the letter, he started another. I said, "Oh no! Not another one!" He said, "I have to write my Dad, don't I, and thank him for picking such a wonderful person to be my mother?"

I never told my parents how I got the idea, but that evening I wrote a letter to my mother telling her of my gratitude and love, and also one to my father thanking him for choosing such a wonderful mother for me.

I knew they would be glad to get the letters. I didn't know how glad until the next summer. We lived in a small town where most people knew one another. I went to the store, and the merchant said, "Those were nice letters you wrote to your parents for Mother's Day." I asked him, "How do you know?" I found that my mother so prized the letters that she carried them in her pocketbook, and, whenever she could get someone to listen, she read parts of the letters to them.

So often we forget to express love and appreciation to those we know best, those who do the most for us. A woman once said to me, "The more I do for my family, the more they seem to expect. If any of them ever said 'thank-you,' I think I'd drop dead."

A word of appreciation and love can mean so much to another. A note of love left on a pillow, or under a plate, or tucked in a mirror, can cause a burst of sunshine in a loved one's heart. A note to a friend, or to someone who has shown us a kindness can cause joy bells to ring for that person.

Trees and Freedom

A tree would seem to be a strange symbol of freedom. It cannot move about as people do. Yet a tree does have something important to tell us about freedom.

In the first place it tells us that a tree is not free to grow unless it is properly rooted. A person is not free to grow in spirit unless his life is properly rooted by faith in God. If we want freedom to live at peace with ourselves, we must be rooted in God's forgiveness. If we want to be free to experience God's power, we must be rooted in a sense of God's presence. If we want to be free to face death with hope, we must be rooted in God's promises.

Too many people want fruits without roots. They want to be free to live as they please, and so they root themselves in temporary pleasures. The result is that, without proper nourishment, they fail to experience the satisfaction they seek.

Again, a tree reminds us that it can only express its freedom to grow by branching out. The roots do not show, but people know they are there because they notice the tree's growth and can enjoy its fruit or rest in its shade. If people claim to be rooted in God, God wants them to show it by branching out in love to their neighbors. Remember: The roots don't show. It is only as we branch out in Christian service that people can sense the roots of faith that are there.

Of course, a tree is not free to make itself grow. Its growth is a response to something. It responds to sun and rain and to the nourishment in the soil. Christian faith too, is a response to something. It responds to God's love in Christ expressed in his life and death on the cross. This is what nourishes the roots of our faith and leads us to branch out in service to our neighbor and in witness to the power of God.

A Cluster of Freedoms

An astronomer once pointed out a star to me. To the naked eye it looked like one star, but through a telescope it appeared to be two stars. Then, through a stronger telescope, I saw that each of these stars was two stars. What I had thought was one star was a cluster of at least four stars.

Freedom in the United States is really a cluster of freedoms: freedom of speech, freedom of assembly, freedom to dissent, and many other freedoms. Not the least of these is the freedom to practice our religion without outside interference or reprisal from the government or any other group.

It is the experience of true Christian believers that Christ sets us free from the dominion of sin, free from guilt, free to feel accepted by God, free to experience inner peace, free to love our neighbors.

This does not mean that a Christian is free to do anything he or she pleases; there is no such thing as absolute freedom. Sooner or later, we run up against the rights of others and against the immutable laws of God. As long as gravitation exists, we are not free to jump off a tall building and live.

Even freedom must run on a track, or it can end up in a crash. In matters of law, that track in the United States is the Constitution. In matters of morals, for millions that track is the Bible. The trouble is that not everyone believes the Bible or interprets it the same way. Among our citizens are many kinds of Christians as well as many who hold to other faiths. That's why, in matters of religion, each person must be free to choose his or her own track. Each, in turn, must grant that same right to others.

But Christ not only frees us *from* something; he frees us *for* something. He frees us to love our neighbor in a new way (Galatians 5:13). As long as we look down on another person, we are not free to love that individual. Christ wants us to be free of hostility and prejudice, so that we will be free to offer the kind of love and goodwill this world so desperately needs.

The Problem of Problems

A certain minister had the habit of practicing his sermons aloud in his study. One day when he went to his study, he found that someone had put a sign on his door saying, "This is where our pastor practices what he preaches."

This, in a way, is what John Wesley called the "problem of problems": how to get Christians to practice what they profess. We talk about love, but sometimes we practice it too little. We talk about forgiveness, but we find it hard to forgive.

The author of the book of James was concerned about this problem. What good does it do, he asks, to say we are Christians if we don't live like Christians? He does not say that good works can replace faith. He does say that our faith should be demonstrated by the way we live.

If our acceptance by God depended upon our good deeds, we never could be sure we were accepted. We would be like a person who said, "I have been working for my salvation for forty years, and I'm not sure yet." This is why Paul was so insistent that our acceptance by God depends upon our faith. After all, the penitent thief on the cross had no good works to show, yet Jesus assured him of acceptance in paradise. His tragedy was that he found faith so late, and lived a wasted life.

Bible ethics have been called "gratitude ethics." The Hebrews were told to obey the Ten Commandments in gratitude that God had led them from bondage in Egypt (Exodus 20:2). Christians are told to practice their faith, not to put God in their debt but because they know they are indebted to God's grace for their acceptance.

In some countries Christians are not permitted to speak of their faith. They can only engage in nonmissionary activities. Their hope is that others will see a difference in them and become curious about what gives them serenity and love in the face of rejection and oppression.

14

The Call to Triumphant Living

We began this book with glimpses that remind us of Christ—of his life, death, and resurrection. We spoke of the hope of eternal life that his resurrection makes possible.

Most of us, however, have a lot of living to do yet on this earth. We want to do it as triumphantly as possible. We don't know what heaven will be like, but we do know what this life is like. We know its sorrows as well as its joys, its failures as well as its successes, its disappointments as well as its fulfillments, its frustrations as well as its victories.

We want a faith that can spur us on in spite of our obstacles, one that can give us a sense of victory in the face of our adversaries. We want a faith for triumphant living.

The testimony of millions is that Christianity offers such a faith. It spurs us on when we are tempted to give up. It tells us we are not alone in facing the rewards and vicissitudes of life. God is with us. Faith in God can give us hope and courage.

The need for a triumphant faith is constant and daily. We need a faith that not only helps us to face the crises of life with courage and conviction but can transform the ordinary routine of daily existence into a sense of excitement and fulfillment: a faith that can help us believe in ourselves and can give us a sense of partnership with God. Here, then, are illustrations that can help us in our quest of a faith for triumphant living.

How's Your Arthritis?

A certain woman liked to go to a certain post office to buy stamps because the postal workers were always so friendly to her. At Christmastime, when the post office was full of people waiting to mail packages, someone explained to her that she did not have to wait in line for stamps because there was a machine that sold stamps. "But, she said sweetly as she remained in line, "the machine doesn't ask me about my arthritis."

Brooks Hays told about a boy who was the largest in his class. Unfortunately, he also had the lowest I.Q. One day, when there were visitors in the class, the teacher said to him, "Otto, will you please raise the window?" As he went to do her bidding, she exclaimed, "I don't know what I'd do without Otto. He's the only boy in the class strong enough to raise that window." Later, she confided to the visitors, "The window didn't need to be raised, but Otto needed to be recognized."

We all need to be recognized. We all want someone to notice us, to pay us the compliment of their attention.

As one minister visited his shut-in members, he always tried to put his hand on one of theirs as he prayed for them. Often he would kiss them on the cheek, because he remembered a lonely woman in a nursing home saying, "No one ever touches me anymore except the nurse."

Machines can never take the place of interpersonal relationships. A machine may keep us from standing in line. It can't ask us how we are. A TV can entertain us, but it cannot put an arm around us or give us a good-night kiss.

So! How's your arthritis?

Staying by the Stuff

Calvary Baptist Church in Washington, D. C., has a men's Bible class known as the Vaughn Bible Class. It was named for its founder, who was very active in religious and civic affairs. His wife stayed in the background. She kept the home, in which young people were always welcome and her husband found love and contentment.

When Mrs. Vaughn died, her funeral service was conducted by the Rev. Homer J. Councilor. For his tribute he chose a most unusual text, but one that Mrs. Vaughn's granddaughter has remembered down through the years. His tribute was, "She stayed by the stuff."

The text was taken from the King James Version of First Samuel. David went up to demand provisions from a wealthy landowner named Nabal. In case there might be trouble, he took four hundred men with him. Two hundred remained behind to guard the camp. They "abode by the stuff" (1 Samuel 25:13). Later, David attacked the Amalekites. Again, he took many soldiers with him and left others to guard the camp. Those who waged the battle did not want to share what they had captured with those who had stayed behind, but David made a rule: "As his part is that goeth down to the battle, so shall his part be that tarrieth by the stuff" (1 Samuel 30:24).

The world needs its explorers, trailblazers, innovative thinkers, and doers. But it also needs those who "stay by the stuff," who guard the old virtues and do the menial tasks that need to be done.

No matter how great the surgeon, nurses are needed to check the temperature, give the medicine, and feed and bathe the patient. No matter how great the artist, suppliers are needed to provide the canvas and paints.

These are the days when women rightfully demand equal recognition in the world of affairs. They have been denied this role for too long. Nevertheless, work within the home is still important. Someone must cook and feed the babies. Housework can, and should be, a shared responsibility. But those who do it deserve the thanks of a grateful world.

The Common Is Not So Common

Few things are more commonplace than a dandelion. If one had a dollar for every dandelion that grows, one could pay off the national debt and have a lot of money left over.

There are some things to be said, though, even for the lowly dandelion. It does have a beautiful color, and it will grow where nothing else will. The dandelion has neither prejudice nor pride. It will grow on a rich person's estate or in a poor person's yard. It will blossom near a palace or on a cinder dump. Rich man, poor man, black or white, it makes no difference to a dandelion. It will grow on any person's property where it gets a chance to root.

Because of its commonness, Jesus would have noticed the dandelion. He was always glorifying the commonplace. Light, salt, lilies, sparrows, all take on new significance because he mentioned them. Labor takes on new dignity because he worked with his hands. Bread and wine take on new significance because he made them symbols of his death. Nothing was too small or insignificant to merit his attention. Jesus pointed out that God notices *us* even more.

In spite of most people's disdain for them, dandelions rise above their surroundings. If the grass is two inches high, dandelion stems will grow three inches. If grass is five inches high, dandelion stems will grow seven.

Some people are like that. They rise above their discouragements and troubles. They live tall because they reach up for the sunshine of God's love and will. They refuse to be smothered by daily routines.

If people could scatter kindness the way a dandelion scatters seed, the world would be surprised at the growth of goodwill. So consider the dandelion! It does add color to some of the drab places of earth.

What Color Are Your Thoughts?

We do not hear just with our ears. We hear with our total background. We hear with our understanding. We hear with our points of view. We hear with our prejudices. We interpret what we hear even while we are hearing it.

Stephen Crane illustrated this fact in an interesting way. If one person, he said, could color all his thoughts blue and another person could color his thoughts yellow, and if the first person put one of his blue thoughts into the other's mind, it would not remain a blue thought in the midst of yellow thoughts. Even as it entered the other person's mind, it would turn green, because it would become mixed with the thoughts that are already there.

When God uses us in his kingdom, it is not like water flowing through a metal pipe, unable to absorb any of the metal through which it flows. It is more like a thought passing through the mind of God. God absorbs our thoughts, talents, faith, and commitment, and uses them to God's glory. We must keep our thoughts clean and train our minds and our talents, so that God can use us more effectively for God's purposes.

The glorious thing is that God uses us at all. Anyone who has ever tried to speak through an interpreter to people of another language knows what a problem it can be. Speaking through an interpreter, Dr. Theodore F. Adams, once said, "The Christian way of life works." The interpreter looked puzzled when he heard "works" and said, "Labors?" Dr. Adams had to rephrase his thought before the interpreter could interpret what he meant.

At best, we are poor interpreters of God. But God still wants us to interpret. God wants to use our faith, our talents, our witness in order to speak through them to others. If we let God, God can color our thoughts and actions with the brilliant hues of love and use them to bless others.

When Life Slams the Door in Our Faces

When I first came to Washington, the eloquent voice of Peter Marshall could still be heard from the pulpit of the New York Avenue Presbyterian Church. Then, at an early age, Peter died of a heart attack. Many of us who were his friends, and who knew the effectiveness of his preaching, could not understand why God would let such an eloquent witness be stilled so soon.

But God knew that his wife Catherine could write. Soon after Peter's death, she was led to pour out her anguish and faith in the book *A Man Called Peter.* By this best-seller and by many other books and articles that would follow, she amplified her husband's message so that it reached out to touch the lives of millions of people who never would have heard Peter's voice if he had lived to preach a thousand years.

Peter believed that when God closed the door of his earthly ministry, he would have a bigger door for him to enter. He used to say that he believed the most exciting five minutes in all eternity would be the first five minutes after death. But Catherine, too, was shown another door. She substituted her pen for Peter's voice, and by that means has blessed the lives of millions of readers.

Sometimes life does slam the door in our face. Often we are tempted to cry out in anger against a God who would let it happen, but God often permits one door to be closed because another door is waiting to be opened. Often faith and loyalty can help us to find that door and go through it to the glory of God.

How to Sleep on a Windy Night

A friend once told me this story. A farmer got too old to farm. So he decided to move into the village and hire a younger man to run the farm. He interviewed an applicant who said he knew how to do farm work. "What do you know how to do best?" the farmer asked him. To his surprise the man answered, "How to sleep on a windy night." It was a strange answer, but the farmer needed his help, so he hired the man.

One night, a fierce storm swept over the area. Remembering what the hired man had said, the farmer jumped into his car and sped out to the farm. He had visions of the hired man sleeping while the cows stood out in the storm and the hay was blown all over the field.

Sure enough, he found the hired man asleep. But the hay was under cover, and the cows were all safely in their stalls. Then he knew why the man could sleep on a windy night. He had done everything he could to get ready for the storm before it came. If he had left any chore undone, he would not have been able to sleep during the storm.

The time to prepare for a storm is before it happens. For a person with an uneasy conscience, every night is a stormy night. Nothing robs us of peace of mind like guilt. Sometimes fear of being found out adds to the worry. There is no untroubled sleep for such a person. Such a person needs to confess his sins and seek forgiveness.

But, assuming we have sought and found peace with God, we must do the best we can and leave the rest up to others and to God. When Jesus said on the cross, "It is finished" (John 19:30), surely he meant that he had done everything God sent him to do.

None of us will ever have that satisfaction. We always have left some things undone. But when we know we have tried to do our best, then we can face the Lord and our conscience with serenity and peace.

Choosing the Right Targets

A stranger was riding through a countryside when he saw a most unusual sight. At various levels on the side of an old barn, he saw several targets, and in the center of every target—right in the bull's-eye—there was an arrow. The stranger was so impressed that he stopped to ask who was such an expert marksman. The farmer replied that no one around there was an expert marksman so far as he knew. "But those arrows," said the stranger. "Every one is right in the bull's-eye."

"Oh," said the farmer, "The village idiot does that. He comes out here and shoots arrows into the side of my barn, and then he seems to get a lot of pleasure out of painting targets around them."

Any person—I almost said any idiot—can do something and then think up reasons or excuses afterward to try to justify his action. But it takes a person with real vision to choose his targets first. He may not always hit the bull's-eye, but how else can he know he is aiming in the right direction, and how else can he improve his aim?

It was said of Jonathan Edwards, "He aimed at nothing but the glory of God." Paul said, "Make love your aim" (1 Corinthians 14:1). Surely he never meant this verse to be separated from the preceding chapter, in which he had discussed the nature of Christian love. This love, he said, is greater even than faith and hope. Then comes what he surely meant to be the punch line, the "therefore": "Make love your aim."

Too often we make pride or self-interest or some less worthy goal our target, but God wants us to aim at love in all that we do.

Real or Artificial?

A woman in Auburn, Maine, received a bouquet of beautiful roses. A neighbor admired the roses with the words: "They are so beautiful, they almost look artificial."

That's a switch. Usually we judge the man-made product by how realistically it imitates the real thing. Was she joking? Was it a slip of the tongue? Or had she seen so many artificial flowers that she had accepted them as her criterion of floral beauty?

Is not this part of our problem? We are so surrounded by man-made products that we have lost our sense of awe before the marvels and mysteries of nature. We are so impressed by human ingenuity that we almost forget God is the supreme artist. God is not only nature's creator, God is also its designer. God is the author of beauty. God created the rose. God gives us the designs to copy. Most of all, God wants us to copy holiness: "Be holy, for I am holy" (Leviticus 11:44). That is the imitation God most wants people to admire in us.

Jesus knew about human resourcefulness. He knew the stories of Solomon's fabulous wealth. Nevertheless, he was more impressed by the beauty of a roadside flower than by all the legends of Solomon's glory. God's creativeness, not man's cleverness, was the basis of his trust.

The Art of Keeping at It

A poem about the Grand Canyon says that the Colorado River has shown what can be done "just by keeping at it." Of course, the nature of the soil helped to make it possible. Other rivers have kept at it without the same result. Nevertheless, it was the constant flow of the Colorado River that carved out one of nature's most spectacular masterpieces.

Perseverance is an extremely important trait. Many of the greatest discoveries have been made by people who refused to give up. Take William Coolidge, for example. Thomas Edison was determined to invent an electric light although almost all major scientists insisted it couldn't be done. He believed he could do so if he could find the right substance to serve as a filament.

That's where William Coolidge came in. For some reason he believed tungsten would provide the answer, but tungsten was very brittle. It crumbled almost at a touch. How could a wire be made from that?

For six years Coolidge persisted in trying to find the answer. Finally, he found a way to make a tungsten wire thinner than a hair and stronger than steel. He told Edison that, if he had known the metallurgy of that day, he would have given up, for he would have believed it couldn't be done. But by dogged persistence he did it.

William Carey was the first Protestant missionary to India. To his nephew he wrote, "If after my removal, any one should think it worth his while to write my life, I will give you a criterion by which you may judge of its correctness. If he gives me credit for being a plodder, he will describe me justly. Anything beyond this will be too much. I can plod. I can persevere in any definite pursuit. To this I owe everything."

One cannot accomplish everything by perseverance, but very little can be accomplished without it. It is the Christian, who keeps on running "with perseverance the race that is set before us" (Hebrews 12:1), who finishes the race.

Bombs and Bibles

The year was 1899. American troops were on the soil of the Philippines. Concerning the people of the islands, Gilbert Pierce, a United States senator from North Dakota, said:

> Most of the brethren that I have heard have been in favor of going forward, as they say, with a Bible in one hand and a gun, or a sword, in the other. Well, this is a favorable time to extend the gospel, and I see that Senator Davis says that we are undoubtedly the consecrated evangelists of humanity. But I am inclined to think that we cannot safely preach to an enemy until we have whipped him, and so I would not take many books just now, but I would take guns in both hands. This need not hinder us from praying for these people's conversions.

Where is the truth of God in such a statement? There may be times—Christians are not agreed on this—when a nation is forced to accept war as the lesser of two evils. But all would surely agree that the militant words of the senator are a far cry from the striking words of Jesus, "But I say to you, Love your enemies, bless them that curse you, do good to them that hate you, and pray for them which despitefully use you, and persecute you" (Matthew 5:44, KJV).

How can we convert an enemy if we have killed him? How can one preach the love of God to him at the end of a gun barrel? It is hard to pray for one's conversion when one is pointing a gun at him. There may be times when the world must curb the utter madness of a person like Hitler by warfare, but we must never think of war as the way to advance the kingdom of God.

Light in a Child's Eyes

Mrs. Henlee Barnette tells a delightful incident concerning her husband, a distinguished theological professor in Louisville, Kentucky. One night it snowed, and since snow does not fall too often in Louisville, Mrs. Barnette went out after breakfast to help her daughter make a snowman.

They were having such a good time that time got away from her, and, when her husband came home for lunch, the unwashed breakfast dishes were still in the sink. She apologized for the messy condition in the kitchen. "I didn't notice," he said, "because I was blinded by the light in our daughter's eyes when I came in."

Blessed is the person who can still see the light in a child's eyes. God forgive us for so often quenching that light. We get too busy, or too tired, or too wrapped up in our own affairs, so we turn children aside when they come to us with their delightful discoveries and eager questions.

A child has a priceless boon—curiosity. Every child is a natural explorer. There is so much to learn—so much that grown-ups take for granted—that every day yields exciting discoveries.

They also have a brand-new imagination. They have not soiled it with sordid thoughts. It populates their world with people and creatures that grown-ups cannot see. Sometimes it makes God very real.

Dr. C. Oscar Johnson used to tell about a little girl who looked at a beautiful sunrise and said, "Good morning, God." Later the father asked, "Why can't I feel that way?"

Children, of course, can sometimes be very difficult. They want their own way, and they want it at once. That is why it is easier for adults to be childish than to be childlike. All that is worst in a child—selfishness, temper—we tend to carry into adulthood. All that is best—trust, love, wide-eyed wonder, eagerness to learn—we sometimes drop along the way. We need to go back and find what we lost so that in God's eyes we can become once again as a little child.

While There Is Time

I had watched a TV documentary about laser beams. It showed how a beam of light can cut through a thick plate of steel. The frightening prediction was made that the laser beam may be developed into a death ray that could completely change the nature of modern warfare.

That night I dreamed I was at a banquet. A man was speaking. Ordinarily, I do not remember my dreams, but I remember this man in my dream saying, "While there is time."

Evidently while I was sleeping, my mind was still dwelling on the peril our world faces today. Unless nations learn to live together in peace *while there is time,* we may all be burned to a crisp.

While there is time! That has always been the cry of those who point to the biblical promise of Christ's Second Coming. Indeed, Jesus himself issued the warning, "Watch therefore, for you do not know on what day your Lord is coming" (Matthew 24:42). Even Jesus worked under the shadow of a limited time. "We must work the works of him that sent me, while it is day; night comes, when no one can work" (John 9:4).

Time is a very precious commodity. No one knows how much of it he has left. Nor does the world know. We dare not postpone putting our trust in the One who transcends time.

Topical Index